Poetic Gems
1st & 2nd Series

by

WILLIAM M^CGONAGALL

The Echo Library 2007

Published by

The Echo Library

Echo Library
131 High St.
Teddington
Middlesex TW11 8HH

www.echo-library.com

Lay out and new editorial content copyright Echo Library 2007

Please report serious faults in the text to complaints@echo-library.com

Isbn 978-1-4068-2341-7

*Faithfully Yours
William McGonagall
Poet, and Tragedian.*

POETIC GEMS

SELECTED FROM THE WORKS

OF

WILLIAM M^CGONAGALL,

Poet and Tragedian

WITH

BIOGRAPHICAL SKETCH AND REMINISCENCES

BY THE AUTHOR,

CONTENTS

	PAGE
Brief Autobiography	1
Reminiscences	8
Tribute to Mr M'Gonagall from Three Students University	14
Ode to William M'Gonagall	15
Tribute from Zululand	17
Testimonials	18
An Ode to the Queen on Her Jubilee Year	19
The Death of Prince Leopold	21
The Death of Lord and Lady Dalhousie	23
The Funeral of the German Emperor	25
The Battle of Tel-el-Kebir	28
The Famous Tay Whale	30
The Railway Bridge of the Silvery Tay	32
The Newport Railway	34
The Tay Bridge Disaster	35
An Address to the New Tay Bridge	37
The Late Sir John Ogilvy	39
The Rattling Boy from Dublin	40
The Burial of the Rev. George Gilfillan	42
The Battle of El-Teb	44
The Battle of Abu Klea	46
A Christmas Carol	48
The Christmas Goose	50
An Autumn Reverie	52
The Wreck of the Steamer "London" while on Australia	54
The Wreck of the "Thomas Dryden" in Pentland Firth	56
Attempted Assassination of the Queen	58
Saving a Train	60
The Moon	62
The Beautiful Sun	63
Grace Darling; or, the Wreck of the "Forfarshire"	65
To Mr James Scrymgeour, Dundee	67
The Battle of Bannockburn	69
Edinburgh	72
Glasgow	73
Oban	75
The Battle of Flodden Field	77
Greenland's Icy Mountains	80
A Tribute to Henry M. Stanley	82
Jottings of New York	84
Beautiful Monikie	86
A Tribute to Mr Murphy and the Blue Ribbon Army	87
Loch Katrine	89

Forget-Me-Not	91
The Royal Review	93
The Nithsdale Widow and Her Son	95
Jack o' the Cudgel: Part I.	98
Part II.	100
The Battle of Culloden	102
The Battle of Sheriffmuir	105
The Execution of James Graham, Marquis of Montrose	107
Baldovan	109
Loch Leven	110
Montrose	111
The Castle of Mains	112
Broughty Ferry	113
Robert Burns	114
Adventures of King Robert the Bruce	115
A Tale of the Sea	117
Descriptive Jottings of London	120
Annie Marshall the Foundling	121
Bill Bowls the Sailor	123
Young Munro the Sailor	125
The Death of the Old Mendicant	127
An Adventure in the Life of King James V. of Scotland	129
The Clepington Catastrophe	131
The Rebel Surprise Near Tamai	133
Burning of the Exeter Theatre	135
John Rouat the Fisherman	137
The Sorrows of the Blind	139
General Gordon, the Hero of Khartoum	140
The Battle of Cressy	142
The Wreck of the Barque "Wm. Paterson," of Liverpool	144
Hanchen, the Maid of the Mill	146
Wreck of the Schooner "Samuel Crawford"	149
The First Grenadier of France	151
The Tragic Death of the Rev. A. H. Mackonochie	153
The Burning of the Steamer "City of Montreal"	155
The Wreck of the Whaler "Oscar"	157
Jenny Carrister, the Heroine of Lucknow-Mine	159
The Horrors of Majuba	161
The Miraculous Escape of Robert Allan, the Fireman	163
The Battle of Shina, in Africa, Fought in 1800	165
The Collision in the English Channel	167
The Wreck of the Steamer "Storm Queen"	169
The Pennsylvania Disaster	171
The Sprig of Moss	173

BRIEF AUTOBIOGRAPHY.

DEAR READER,—My parents were both born in Ireland, where they spent the great part of their lives after their marriage. They left Ireland for Scotland, and never returned to the Green Isle. I was born in the year of 1830 in the city of Edinburgh, the garden of bonnie Scotland, which is justly famed by all for its magnificent scenery. My parents were poor, but honest, sober, and God-fearing. My father was a hand-loom weaver, and wrought at cotton fabrics during his stay in Edinburgh, which was for about two years. Owing to the great depression in the cotton trade in Edinburgh, he removed to Paisley with his family, where work was abundant for a period of about three years; but then a crash taking place, he was forced to remove to Glasgow with his family with the hope of securing work there, and enable him to support his young and increasing family, as they were all young at that time, your humble servant included. In Glasgow he was fortunate in getting work as a cotton weaver; and as trade was in a prosperous state for about two years, I was sent to school, where I remained about eighteen months, but at the expiry of which, trade again becoming dull, my poor parents were compelled to take me from school, being unable to pay for schooling through adverse circumstances; so that all the education I received was before I was seven years of age.

My father, being forced to leave Glasgow through want of work, came to Dundee, where plenty of work was to be had at the time— such as sacking, cloth, and other fabrics. It was at this time that your humble servant was sent to work in a mill in the Scouringburn, which was owned by Mr Peter Davie, and there I remained for about four years, after which I was taken from the mill, and put to learn the handloom in Ex-Provost Reid's factory, which was also situated in the Scouringburn. After I had learned to be an expert hand-loom weaver, I began to take a great delight in reading books, as well as to improve my handwriting, in my leisure hours at night, until I made myself what I am.

The books that I liked best to read were Shakspeare's penny plays, more especially Macbeth, Richard III., Hamlet, and Othello; and I gave myself no rest until I obtained complete mastery over the above four characters. Many a time in my dear father's absence I enacted entire scenes from Macbeth and Richard III., along with some of my shopmates, until they were quite delighted; and many a time they regaled me and the other actors that had entertained them to strong ale, biscuits, and cheese.

My first appearance on any stage was in Mr Giles' theatre, which was in Lindsay Street quarry, some years ago: I cannot give the exact date, but it is a very long time ago. The theatre was built of brick, somewhat similar to Mr M'Givern's at the top of Seagate. The character that I appeared in was Macbeth, Mrs Giles sustaining the character of Lady Macbeth on that occasion, which she performed admirably. The way that I was allowed to perform was in terms of the following agreement, which was entered into between Mr Giles and myself—that I had to give Mr Giles one pound in cash before the performance, which I considered rather hard, but as there was no help for it, I made known Mr Giles's terms to my shopmates, who were handloom weavers in Seafield Works, Taylor's Lane. No sooner than the terms were made known to them, than they entered heartily into the arrangement, and in a very short time they made up the pound by subscription, and with one accord declared they would go and see me perform the Thane of Fife, *alias* Macbeth. To see that the arrangement with Mr Giles was carried out to the letter, a deputation of two of my shopmates was appointed to wait upon him with the pound. Mr Giles received the deputation, and on receipt of the money cheerfully gave a written agreement certifying that he would allow me to perform Macbeth on the following night in his theatre. When the deputation came back with the news that Mr Giles had consented to allow me to make my *debut* on the following night, my shopmates cheered again and again, and the rapping of the lays I will never forget as long as I live. When the great night arrived my shopmates were in high glee with the hope of getting a Shakspearian treat from your humble servant. And I can assure you, without boasting, they were not disappointed in their anticipations, my shopmates having secured seats before the general public were admitted. It would be impossible for me to describe the scene in Lindsay Street, as it was crowded from head to foot, all being eager to witness my first appearance as an exponent of Shakspeare. When I appeared on the stage I was received with a perfect storm of applause, but when I exclaimed "Command, they make a halt upon the heath," the applause was deafening, and was continued during the entire evening, especially so in the combat scene. The house was crowded during each of the three performances on that ever-memorable night, which can never be forgot by me or my shopmates, and even entire strangers included. At the end of each performance I was called before the curtain, and received plaudit after plaudit of applause in recognition of my able impersonation of Macbeth.

What a sight it was to see such a mass of people struggling to gain admission! hundreds failing to do so, and in the struggle numbers were trampled under foot, one man having lost one of his shoes in the scrimmage; others were carried bodily into the theatre along with the press. So much then for the true account of my first appearance on any stage.

The most startling incident in my life was the time I discovered myself to be a poet, which was in the year 1877. During the Dundee holiday week, in the bright and balmy month of June, when trees and flowers were in full bloom, while lonely and sad in my room, I sat thinking about the thousands of people who were away by rail and steamboat, perhaps to the land of Burns, or poor ill-treated Tannahill, or to gaze upon the Trossachs in Rob Roy's country, or elsewhere wherever their minds led them. Well, while pondering so, I seemed to feel as it were a strange kind of feeling stealing over me, and remained so for about five minutes. A flame, as Lord Byron has said, seemed to kindle up my entire frame, along with a strong desire to write poetry; and I felt so happy, so happy, that I was inclined to dance, then I began to pace backwards and forwards in the room, trying to shake off all thought of writing poetry; but the more I tried, the more strong the sensation became. It was so strong, I imagined that a pen was in my right hand, and a voice crying, "Write Write!" So I said to myself, ruminating, let me see; what shall I write? then all at once a bright idea struck me to write about my best friend, the late Reverend George Gilfillan; in my opinion I could not have chosen a better subject, therefore I immediately found paper, pen, and ink, and set myself down to immortalize the great preacher, poet, and orator. These are the lines I penned, which I dropped into the box of the *Weekly News* office surreptitiously, which appeared in that paper as follows:—

"W. M'G., Dundee, who modestly seeks to hide his light under a bushel, has surreptitiously dropped into our letter-box an address to the Rev. George Gilfillan. Here is a sample of this worthy's powers of versification:—

'Rev. George Gilfillan of Dundee,
   There is none can you excel;
You have boldly rejected the Confession of Faith,
   And defended your cause right well.

'The first time I heard him speak,
   'Twas in the Kinnaird Hall,
Lecturing on the Garibaldi movement,
   As loud as he could bawl.

'He is a liberal gentleman
   To the poor while in distress,
And for his kindness unto them
   The Lord will surely bless.

'My blessing on his noble form,
   And on his lofty head,
May all good angels guard him while living,
   And hereafter when he's dead.'"

P.S.—This is the first poem that I composed while under the divine inspiration, and is true, as I have to give an account to God at the day of judgment for all the sins I have committed.

With regard to my far-famed Balmoral journey, I will relate it truly as it happened. 'Twas on a bright summer morning in the month of July 1878, I left Dundee *en route* for Balmoral, the Highland home of Her Most Gracious Majesty, Queen of Great Britain and Empress of India. Well, my first stage for the day was the village of Alyth. When I arrived there I felt weary, foot-sore, and longed for rest and lodgings for the night. I made enquiry for a good lodging-house, and found one very easily, and for the lodging I paid fourpence to the landlady before I sat down, and when I had rested my weary limbs for about five minutes I rose and went out to purchase some provisions for my supper and breakfast—some bread, tea, sugar, and butter—and when I had purchased the provisions I returned to my lodgings and prepared for myself a hearty tea, which I relished very much, I can assure you, for I felt very hungry, not having tasted food of any kind by the way during the travel, which caused me to have a ravenous appetite, and to devour it greedily; and after supper I asked the landlady to oblige me with some water to wash my feet, which she immediately and most cheerfully supplied me with; then I washed my sore blistered feet and went to bed, and was soon in the arms of Morpheus, the god of sleep. Soundly I slept all the night, until the landlady awoke me in the morning, telling me it was a fine sunshiny morning. Well, of course I arose, and donned my clothes, and I felt quite refreshed after the refreshing sleep I had got during the night; then I gave myself a good washing, and afterwards prepared my breakfast, which I devoured quickly, and left the lodging-house, bidding the landlady good morning, and thanking her for her kindness then I wended my way the next day as far as the Spittal o' Glenshee—

> Which is the most dismal to see—
> With its bleak, rocky mountains,
> And clear, crystal fountains,
> With their misty foam;
> And thousands of sheep there together do roam,
> Browsing on the barren pasture, blasted-like to see,
> Stunted in heather, and scarcely a tree;
> And black-looking cairns of stones, as monuments to show,
> Where people have been found that were lost in the snow—
> Which is cheerless to behold—
> And as the traveller gazes thereon it makes his blood run cold,
> And almost makes him weep,
> For a human voice is seldom heard there,
>
> Save the shepherd crying to his sheep.
> The chain of mountains there is most frightful to see,
> Along each side of the Spittal o' Glenshee;
> But the Castleton o' Braemar is most beautiful to see,
> With its handsome whitewashed houses, and romantic scenery,
> And bleak-looking mountains, capped with snow,
> Where the deer and the roe do ramble to and fro,
> Near by the dark river Dee,
> Which is most beautiful to see.
>
> And Balmoral Castle is magnificent to be seen,
> Highland home of the Empress of India, Great Britain's Queen,
> With its beautiful pine forests, near by the river Dee,
> Where the rabbits and hares do sport in mirthful glee,
> And the deer and the roe together do play
> All the live long summer day,
> In sweet harmony together,
> While munching the blooming heather,
> With their hearts full of glee,
> In the green woods of Balmoral, near by the river Dee.

And, my dear friends, when I arrived at the Spittal o' Glenshee, a dreadful thunderstorm came on, and the vivid flashes of the forked lightning were fearful to behold, and the rain poured down in torrents, until I was drenched to the skin, and longed to be under cover from the pitiless rain. Still God gave me courage to proceed on my weary journey, until I arrived at a shepherd's house near by the wayside, and I called at the house, as God had directed me to do, and knocked at the door fearlessly. I was answered by the servant maid, who asked me kindly what I wanted, and I told her I wanted lodgings for the night, and that I was wet to the skin with the rain, and that I felt cold and hungry, and that I would feel thankful for any kind of shelter for the night, as it was still raining and likely to be for the night. Then she told me there was no accommodation; then the shepherd himself came to the door, and he asked me what I wanted, and I told him I wanted a lodging for the night, and at first he seemed unwilling, eyeing me with a suspicious look, perhaps taking me for a burglar, or a sheep-stealer, who had come to steal his sheep—at least that was my impression. But when I showed him Her Most Gracious Majesty's royal letter, with the royal black seal, that I had received from her for my poetic abilities, he immediately took me by the hand and bade me come in, and told me to "gang in ower to the fire and to warm mysel'," at the same time bidding the servant maid make some supper ready for the poet; and while the servant girl was making some porridge for me, I showed him a copy of my poems, which I gave to him as a present for his kindness towards me, which he read during the time I was taking my supper, and seemed to appreciate very much. Then when I had taken my supper, he asked me if I would be afraid to sleep in the barn, and I told him so long as I put my trust in God I had nought to fear, and that these were the principles my dear parents had taught me. When I told him so he felt quite delighted, and bade me warm my feet before I would "gang oot to my bed i' the barn," and when I had warmed my feet, he accompanied me to the barn, where there was a bed that might have pleased Her Most Gracious Majesty, and rolling down the bed-clothes with his own hands, he wished me a sound sleep, and bade me good night. Then I instantly undressed and tumbled into bed, and was soon sound asleep, dreaming that I saw Her Most Gracious Majesty riding in her carriage-and-pair, which was afterwards truly verified. Well, when I awoke the next morning I felt rather chilled, owing to the wetting I had got, and the fatigue of the distance I had travelled; but, nothing daunted, I still resolved to see Her Majesty. So I dressed myself quickly, and went over to the house to bid the shepherd good morning, and thank him for the kindness I had received at his hands, but I was told by the girl he was away tending the sheep, but that he had told her to give me my breakfast, and she bade me come in and sit down and get it. So of course I went in, and got a good breakfast of porridge and good Highland milk, enough to make a hungry soul to sing with joy, especially in a strange country, and far from home. Well, having breakfasted, I arose and bade the servant girl good-bye, at the same time thanking her and the shepherd—her master—for their kindness towards me. Then, taking to the road again, I soon came in sight of the Castleton o' Braemar, with its beautiful whitewashed houses and romantic scenery, which I have referred to in my poem. When I arrived at the Castleton o' Braemar it was near twelve o'clock noon, and from the Castleton it is twelve miles to Balmoral; and I arrived at the lodge gates of the palace of Balmoral just as the tower clock chimed three; and when I crossed the little bridge that spans the river Dee, which has been erected by Her Majesty, I walked boldly forward and knocked loudly at the porter lodge door, and it was immediately answered by the two constables that are there night and day, and one of them asked me in a very authoritative tone what

I wanted, and of course I told him I wanted to see Her Majesty, and he repeated, "Who do you want to see?" and I said I was surprised to think that he should ask me again after telling him distinctly that I wanted to see Her Majesty. Then I showed him Her Majesty's royal letter of patronage for my poetic abilities, and he read it, and said it was not Her Majesty's letter; and I said "Who's is it then? do you take me for a forger?" Then he said Sir Thomas Biddulph's signature was not on the letter, but I told him it was on the envelope, and he looked and found it to be so. Then he said, "Why didn't you tell me that before?" I said I forgot. Then he asked me what I wished him to do with the letter, and I requested him to show it to Her Majesty or Sir Thomas Biddulph. He left me, pretending to go up to the palace with the letter, standing out in the cold in front of the lodge, wondering if he would go up to the palace as he pretended. However, be that as it may, I know not, but he returned with an answer as follows:—"Well, I've been up at the Castle with your letter, and the answer I got for you is they cannot be bothered with you," said with great vehemence. "Well," I replied, "it cannot be helped"; and he said it could not, and began to question me when I left Dundee, and the way I had come from Dundee, and where I had lodged by the way; and I told him, and he noted it all down in his memorandum book, and when he had done so he told me I would have to go back home again the same way I came; and then he asked me if I had brought any of my poetry with me, and I said I had, and showed him the second edition, of which I had several copies, and he looked at the front of it, which seemed to arrest his attention, and said, "You are not poet to Her Majesty; Tennyson's the real poet to Her Majesty." Then I said, "Granted; but, sir, you cannot deny that I have received Her Majesty's patronage." Then he said, "I should like very well to hear you give some specimens of your abilities," and I said, "Where?" and he said, "Just where you stand"; and I said, "No, sir, nothing so degrading in the open air. When I give specimens of my abilities it is either in a theatre or some hall, and if you want to hear me take me inside of the lodge, and pay me before I begin; then you shall hear me. These are my conditions, sir; do you accept my terms?" Then he said, "Oh, you might to oblige the young lady there." So I looked around to see the young lady he referred to, and there she was, looking out at the lodge entrance; and when I saw her I said, "No, sir, I will not; if it were Her Majesty's request I wouldn't do it in the open air, far less do it to please the young lady." Then the lady shut the lodge door, and he said, "Well, what do you charge for this book of poems?" and I said "2d.," and he gave it me, telling me to go straight home and not to think of coming back again to Balmoral. So I bade him good-bye and retraced my steps in search of a lodging for the night, which I obtained at the first farmhouse I called at; and when I knocked at the door I was told to come in and warm my feet at the fire, which I accordingly did, and when I told the good wife and man who I was, and about me being at the palace, they felt very much for me, and lodged me for the night, and fed me likewise, telling me to stay with them for a day or two, and go to the roadside and watch Her Majesty, and speak to her, and that I might be sure she would do something for me, but I paid no heed to their advice. And when I had got my supper, I was shown out to the barn by the gudeman, and there was prepared for me a bed which might have done a prince, and the gudeman bade me good night. So I closed the barn door and went to bed, resolving to be up very early the next morning and on the road, and with the thought thereof I couldn't sleep. So as soon as daylight appeared,

I got up and donned my clothes, and went to the farmer's door and knocked, for they had not arisen, it being so early, and I bade them good-bye, thanking them at the same time for their kindness; and in a few minutes I was on the road again for Dundee—it being Thursday morning I refer to—and lodging in the same houses on my homeward journey, which I accomplished in three days, by arriving in Dundee on Saturday early in the day, foot-sore and weary, but not the least discouraged. So ends my ever-memorable journey to Balmoral.

My next adventure was going to New York, America, in the year 1887, March the 10th. I left Glasgow on board the beautiful steamer "Circassia," and had a very pleasant voyage for a fortnight at sea; and while at sea I was quite a favourite amongst the passengers, and displayed my histrionic abilities, to the delight of the passengers, but received no remuneration for so doing; but I was well pleased with the diet I received; also with the kind treatment I met with from the captain and chief steward—Mr Hendry. When I arrived at Castle Garden, New York, I wasn't permitted to pass on to my place of destination until the officials there questioned me regarding the place in New York I was going to, and how old I was, and what trade I was; and, of course, I told them I was a weaver, whereas if I had said I was a poet, they wouldn't allowed me to pass, but I satisfied them in their interrogations, and was allowed to pass on to my place of destination. During my stay in New York with a Dundee man, I tried occasionally to get an engagement from theatrical proprietors and music-hall proprietors, but alas! 'Twasall in vain, for they all told me they didn't encourage rivalry, but if I had the money to secure a hall to display my abilities, or a company of my own, I would make lots of money; but I am sorry to say I had neither, therefore I considered wisely it was time to leave, so I wrote home to a Dundee gentleman requesting him to take me home, and he granted my request cheerfully, and secured for me a passage on board the "Circassia" again, and I had a very pleasant return voyage home again to bonnie Dundee. Since I came home to Dundee I have been very well treated by the more civilised community, and have made several appearances before the public in Baron Zeigler's circus and Transfield's circus, to delighted and crowded audiences; and the more that I was treated unkindly by a few ignorant boys and the Magistrates of the city, nevertheless my heart still clings to Dundee; and, while in Glasgow, my thoughts, night and day, were always towards Dundee; yet I must confess, during a month's stay in Glasgow, I gave three private entertainments to crowded audiences, and was treated like a prince by them, but owing to declining health, I had to leave the city of Glasgow. Since this Book of Poems perhaps will be my last effort,—

> I earnestly hope the inhabitants of the beautiful city of Dundee
> Will appreciate this little volume got up by me,
> And when they read its pages, I hope it will fill their hearts with delight,
> While seated around the fireside on a cold winter's night;
> And some of them, no doubt, will let a silent tear fall
> In dear remembrance of
>
> WILLIAM M'GONAGALL.

REMINISCENCES.

MY DEARLY BELOVED READERS,—I will begin with giving an account of my experiences amongst the publicans. Well, I must say that the first man who threw peas at me was a publican, while I was giving an entertainment to a few of my admirers in a public-house in a certain little village not far from Dundee; but, my dear friends, I wish it to be understood that the publican who threw the peas at me was not the landlord of the public-house, he was one of the party who came to hear me give my entertainment. Well, my dear readers, it was while I was singing my own song, "The Rattling Boy from Dublin Town," that he threw the peas at me. You must understand that the Rattling Boy was courting a lass called Biddy Brown, and the Rattling Boy chanced to meet his Biddy one night in company with another lad called Barney Magee, which, of course, he did not like to see, and he told Biddy he considered it too bad for her to be going about with another lad, and he would bid her good-bye for being untrue to him. Then Barney Magee told the Rattling Boy that Biddy Brown was his lass, and that he could easily find another—and come and have a glass, and be friends. But the Rattling Boy told Barney Magee to give his glass of strong drink to the devil! meaning, I suppose, it was only fit for devils to make use of, not for God's creatures. Because, my friends, too often has strong drink been the cause of seducing many a beautiful young woman away from her true lover, and from her parents also, by a false seducer, which, no doubt, the Rattling Boy considered Barney Magee to be. Therefore, my dear friends, the reason, I think, for the publican throwing the peas at me is because I say, to the devil with your glass, in my song, "The Rattling Boy from Dublin," and he, no doubt, considered it had a teetotal tendency about it, and, for that reason, he had felt angry, and had thrown the peas at me.

My dear readers, my next adventure was as follows:—During the Blue Ribbon Army movement in Dundee, and on the holiday week of the New-year, I was taken into a public-house by a party of my friends and admirers, and requested to give them an entertainment, for which I was to be remunerated by them. Well, my friends, after the party had got a little refreshment, and myself along with the rest, they proposed that I should give them a little entertainment, which I most willingly consented to do, knowing I would be remunerated by the company for so doing, which was the case; the money I received from them I remember amounted to four shillings and sixpence. All had gone on as smoothly as a marriage bell, and every one of the party seemed to be highly delighted with the entertainment I had given them. Of course, you all ought to know that while singing a good song, or giving a good recitation, it helps to arrest the company's attention from the drink; yes! in many cases it does, my friends. Such, at least, was the case with me—at least the publican thought so —for—what do you think?—he devised a plan to bring my entertainment to an end abruptly, and the plan was, he told the waiter to throw a wet towel at me, which, of course, the waiter did, as he was told, and I received the wet towel, full force, in the face, which staggered me no doubt, and had the desired effect of putting an end to me giving any more entertainments in his house. But, of course, the company I had been entertaining felt angry with the publican for being guilty of such a base action towards me, and I felt indignant myself, my friends, and accordingly I left the company I had been entertaining and bade them good-bye. My dear friends, a publican is a creature that would wish to decoy all the money out of the people's pockets that enter his house; he does not want them to give any of their money away for an intellectual entertainment. No, no! by no means; give it all to him, and crush out entertainments altogether, thereby he would make more money if he could only do so. My dear friends, if there were more theatres in society than public-houses, it would be a much better world to live in, at least more moral; and oh! my dear friends, be advised by me. Give your money to the baker, and the butcher, also the shoemaker and the clothier, and shun the publicans; give them no money at all, for this sufficient reason, they would most willingly deprive us of all moral entertainment if we would be as silly as to allow them. They would wish us to think only about what sort of strong drink we should make use of, and to place our affections on that only, and give the most of our earnings to them; no matter whether your families starve or not, or go naked or shoeless; they care not, so as their own families are well clothed from the cold, and well fed. My dear friends, I most sincerely entreat of you to shun the publicans as you would shun the devil, because nothing good can emanate from indulging in strong drink, but only that which is evil. Turn ye, turn ye! why be a slave to the bottle? Turn to God, and He will save you.

>I hope the day is near at hand,
>When strong drink will be banished from our land.

I remember a certain publican in the city that always pretended to have a great regard for me. Well, as I chanced to be passing by his door one day he was standing in the doorway, and he called on me to come inside, and, as he had been in the habit of buying my poetry, he asked me if I was getting on well, and, of course, I told him the truth, that I was not getting on very well, that I had nothing to do, nor I had not been doing anything for three weeks past, and, worse than all, I had no poetry to sell. Then he said that was a very bad job, and that he was very sorry to hear it, and he asked me how much I would take to give an entertainment in his large back-room, and I told him the least I would take would be five shillings. Oh! very well, he replied, I will invite some of my friends and acquaintances for Friday night first, and mind, you will have to be here at seven o'clock punctual to time, so as not to keep the company waiting. So I told him I would remember the time, and thanked him for his kindness, and bade him good-bye. Well, when Friday came, I was there punctually at seven o'clock, and, when I arrived, he told me I was just in time, and that there was a goodly company gathered to hear me. So he bade me go ben to the big room, and that he would be ben himself—as I supposed more to look after the money than to hear me give my entertainment. Well, my readers, when I made my appearance before the company I was greeted with applause, and they told me they had met together for the evening to hear me give my entertainment. Then a round of drink was called for, and the publican answered the call. Some of the company had whisky to drink, and others had porter or ale, whichever they liked best; as for myself, I remember I had ginger beer. Well, when we had all partaken of a little drink, it was proposed by some one in the company that a chairman should be elected for the evening, which seemed to meet with the publican's approbation. Then the chairman was elected, and I was introduced to the company by the chairman as the great poet M'Gonagall, who was going to give them an entertainment from his own productions; hoping they would keep good order and give me a fair hearing, and, if they would, he was sure I would please them. And when he had delivered himself so, he told me to begin, and accordingly I did so, and entertained the company for about an hour and a half. The company was highly satisfied with the entertainment I gave them, and everyone in the company gave three-pence each, or sixpence each—whatever they liked, I suppose—until it amounted to five shillings. Then the chairman told the publican that five shillings had been subscribed anent the entertainment I had given, and handed it to him. Then the publican gave it to me, and I thanked him and the company for the money I received from them anent the entertainment I had given them. Then the chairman proposed that I should sing "The Rattling Boy from Dublin" over again, and that would conclude the evening's entertainment, and that I would get another subscription, which was unanimously carried by the company, but opposed by the publican; and he told me and the company I had no right to get any more than I had bargained for. But, my friends, his motive for objecting to me getting any more money was to get-it himself anent another round of drink he guessed the party would have after I left. And such was the case, as I was told by one of the party the next day, who stayed well up to eleven o'clock, and it was after ten o'clock when I left. Now, my friends, here was a man, a publican, 1 may say, that pretended to be my friend, that was not satisfied with the money that he got from the company for so many rounds of drink, all through me, of course, that had brought them there to hear me give an entertainment. My opinion is, if I had been as simple to have spent my five shillings that I got for giving my entertainment, he would not have felt satisfied either. In my opinion, he would have laughed at my simplicity for doing so. May heaven protect me from all such friends for ever, and protect everyone that reads my experiences amongst the publicans in this little Book of Poetic Gems!

I remember another night while giving an entertainment in a certain public-house to my admirers, and as soon as the publican found out I was getting money for giving the entertainment, he immediately wrote a letter and addressed it to me, or caused some one else to do it for him, and one of the waiters gave it to me. As soon as I received it in my hand I gave it to one of the company to read, and before he broke open the letter I told him it was a hoax, in my opinion, got up to make me leave his house; and, my dear friends, it was just as I thought—a hoax. I was told in that letter, by particular request, to go to Gray's Hall, where a ball was held that evening, and, at the request of the master of the ceremonies, I was requested to come along to the hall, and recite my famous poem, "Bruce of Bannockburn" and I would be remunerated for it, and to hire a cab immediately, for the company at the ball were all very anxious to hear me. So I left the public-house directly, but I was not so foolish as to hire a cab to take me to Gray's Hall. No, my friends, I walked all the way, and called at the hall and shewed the letter to a man that was watching the hall door, and requested him to read it, and to show it to the master of the ball ceremonies, to see if I was wanted to recite my poem, "Bruce of Bannockburn." So the man took the letter from me and shewed it to the master of the ceremonies, and he soon returned with the letter, telling me it was a hoax, which I expected. My dear friends, this lets you see so far, as well as me, that these publicans that won't permit singing or reciting in their houses are the ones that are selfish or cunning. They know right well that while anyone is singing a song in the company, or reciting, it arrests the attention of the audience from off the drink. That is the reason, my dear friends, for the publican not allowing moral entertainments to be carried on in their houses, which I wish to impress on your minds. It is not for the sake of making a noise in their houses, as many of them say by way of an excuse. No! believe me, they know that pleasing entertainment arrests the attention of their customers from off the drink for the time being, and that is the chief reason for them not permitting it, and, from my own experience, I know it to be the case.

I remember another night while in a public-house. This was on a Saturday night, and the room I was in was quite full, both of men and women, and, of course, I was well known to the most of them. However, I was requested to sing them a song, or give them a recitation, which, of course, I consented to do on one condition, that I was paid for it, which the company agreed to do. So accordingly I sang "The Rattling Boy from Dublin," which was well received by the company. Then they proposed I should recite my Bannockburn poem, which I did, and after I had finished, and partaken of a little refreshment, the company made up for me a handsome collection. Then I began to think it was time for me to leave, as they seemed rather inclined to sing and enjoy themselves. However, when I got up to leave the company, I missed my stick. Lo and behold! it was gone from the place I had left it, and was nowhere to be seen by me or anyone else in the company. And white I was searching for it, and making a great fuss about it, one of the waiters chanced to come in with drink to the company, and he told me it had been taken away; for what purpose, my friends, if you know not, I will tell you: to make me leave the house, because I was getting too much money from the company, and the landlady guessed I would leave the house when I missed my stick, which was really the case.

I remember another Saturday night I was in the same public-house, and I was entertaining a number of gentlemen, and had received a second collection of money from them, and as soon as the landlady found out I was getting so much money, she rushed into the room and ordered me out at once, telling me to "hook it" out of here, and laid hold of me by the arm and showed me to the door.

Another case, I remember, happened to me in Perth; worse, in my opinion, than that. Well, my friends, I chanced to be travelling at the time, and, being in very poor circumstances, I thought I would call at a public-house where I was a little acquainted with the landlord, and ask him if he would allow me to give an entertainment in one of his rooms, and I would feel obliged to him if he would be so kind. Well, however, he consented with a little flattery. Sometimes flattery does well; and in reference to flattery I will quote the beautiful lines of John Dryden the poet:—

> "Flattery, like ice, our footing does betray,
> Who can tread sure on the smooth slippery way?
> Pleased with the fancy, we glide swiftly on,
> And see the dangers which we cannot shun."

The entertainment was to come off that night, and to commence at eight o'clock. So, my friends, I travelled around the city—God knows, tired, hungry, and footsore—inviting the people to come and hear me give my entertainment; and, of course, a great number of rich men and poor men came to hear me, and the room was filled by seven o'clock. But, remember, my dear friends, when I wanted to begin, the publican would not allow me until he had almost extracted every penny from the pockets of the company. And when he told me to begin, I remember I felt very reluctant to do so, for I knew I would get but a small recompense for my entertainment. And it just turned out to be as I expected. My dear friends, I only received eighteen-pence for my entertainment from, I daresay, about sixty of a company. I ask of you, my dear readers, how much did the publican realise from the company that night by selling drink? In my opinion, the least he would have realised would be eighteen shillings or a pound. But, depend upon it, they will never take the advantage of me again.

My dear friends, I entreat of you all, for God's sake and for the furtherance of Christ's kingdom, to abstain from all kinds of intoxicating liquor, because seldom any good emanates from it. In the first place, if it was abolished, there would not be so much housebreaking, for this reason: When the burglar wants to break into a house, if he thinks he hasn't got enough courage to do so, he knows that if he takes a few glasses of either rum, whisky, or brandy, it will give him the courage to rob and kill honest disposed people. Yet the Government tolerates such a demon, I may call it, to be sold in society; to help burglars and thieves to rob and kill; also to help the seducer to seduce our daughters; and to help to fill our prisons, and our lunatic asylums, and our poorhouses. Therefore, for these few sufficient reasons, I call upon you, fathers and mothers, and the friends of Christianity, and the friends of humanity,

> To join each one, with heart and hand,
> And help to banish the bane of society from our land,
> And trust in God, and worship Him,
> And denounce the publicans, because they cause sin;
> Therefore cease from strong drink,
> And you will likely do well,
> Then there's not so much danger of going to hell!

My dear friends, along with my experiences amongst the publicans, I will relate to you a rather dangerous adventure that happened to me some years ago, as follows. Being on travel in the parish of Liff, that is, I think, about six miles from Dundee, and as I was very hard up for money at the time, and being rather at a loss how to get a little of that filthy lucre, as some people term it. But, my dear readers, I never considered it to be either filthy or bad. Money is most certainly the most useful commodity in society that I know of. It is certainly good when not abused; but, if abused, the fault rests with the abuser —the money is good nevertheless. For my own part, I have always found it to be one of my best friends. Well, being near to a smithy at the time I refer to, I resolved to call on the smith at the smithy and ask his permission to be allowed to give an entertainment from my own works in the smithy that same night. And when I called on the smith and asked his permission to give my entertainment, and told him who I was, he granted me permission of the smithy cheerfully to give my entertainment. So I went from house to house in the district, inviting the people to come to my entertainment, which was to commence at eight o'clock. Admission—adults, twopence each; children, one penny each. When it drew near to eight o'clock there was a very respectable audience gathered to hear me, and gave me a very hearty welcome and a patient hearing; and they all felt highly delighted with the entertainment I had given them, and many of them inviting me to hurry back again, and give them another entertainment. The proceeds, I remember, for the entertainment I gave amounted to four shillings and ninepence, which I was very thankful for. Well, my dear friends, after I had thanked the smith for the liberty of his smithy, and had left and had drawn near to Liff schoolroom, I heard the pattering of men's feet behind me, and an undefinable fear seized me. Having my umbrella with me I grasped it firmly, and waited patiently until three men came up to me near Liff school-room, and there they stood glaring at me as the serpent does before it leaps upon its prey. Then the man in the centre of the three whispered to his companions, and, as he did so, he threw out both his hands, with the intention, no doubt, of knocking me down, and, with the assistance of the other two, robbing me of the money I had realised from my entertainment. But when he threw out his arms to catch hold of me, as quick as lightning I struck him a blow across the legs with my umbrella, which made him leap backwards, and immediately they then went away round to the front of the school-master's house, close by the road side, and planted themselves there. And when I saw they were waiting for me to come that way as they expected, I resolved to make my escape from them the best way I could. But how? ah, that was the rub. However, I went round to the front of the school-master's house, and reviewed them in the distance, and, the night being dark, the idea struck me if I could manage to get away from their sight they would give up the chase, and go home to Lochee without satisfying their evil intentions. Well, my friends, the plan I adopted was by lowering my body slowly downwards until my knees were touching the ground, and, in that position, I remained for a few seconds; then I threw myself flat on my face on the road, and I remained in that way watching them in the greatest fear imaginable. But, thank God the plan I adopted had the desired effect of saving me from being robbed, or perhaps murdered. Then I thought it advisable to go home by Birkhill, for fear of meeting the night poachers or prowlers again. And when I arrived at Birkhill I resolved to go home by passing through Lord Duncan's woods. I considered it would be safer doing so than by going home the way the poachers had gone, and, just as I made my entry into Lord Duncan's woods, I began to sing—

> Yea, though I walk in death's dark vale,
>   Yet will I fear none ill,
> For Thou art with me, and Thy rod
>   And staff me comfort still.

So, my dear readers, I arrived safe home, and thanked God for delivering me from the hands of evil-doers, as He has done on all occasions.

TRIBUTE FROM THREE STUDENTS AT GLASGOW UNIVERSITY.

The University,
Glasgow, February 1891.

To William M'Gonagall,'
  Poet and Tragedian,
    City of Dundee.

Dear Sir,—We, the undersigned, beg to send you herewith an Ode we have composed in your honour. We have had the extreme pleasure of reading your "Poetic Gems," and have embodied our sentiments in the poem referred to. We do not hope to receive a very favourable criticism upon our small effort, but as young men desirous to imitate the master of poetic art we have discovered in you, we trust you will be as lenient as possible with your enthusiastic disciples. We do not wish to rival your splendid achievements, as that would be as presumptuous as it would be futile, but if we can, afar off, emulate the performances of the poet of Dundee, or in a remote way catch any of his inspiration, our reward will be truly great. We beg, therefore, that you will write us, and inform us what you think of our poem. You might also reply, as far as you are able, to the following questions:—

    I. What grammar would you recommend as a preliminary study to the writing of poetry?
    II. Is a College education an aid to write poetry, and what University would you recommend?
    III. Is the most intellectual benefit to be derived from a study of the M'Gonagallian or Shakespearian school of poetry?
    IV. Does your own success in the realms of poetry enable you to estimate what special capacity any of us may have for lyric poetry or the drama?
    V. Would you recommend any of us to try our chance at the histrionic art; and if not, why not? Is Macbeth or Richard III. the best character to take up?
    VI. Would you recommend us to write direct to the Queen as a patron of poetry; or should we go to Balmoral to see her there?
    VII. What chances do you consider we have in knocking out Tennyson as Poet Laureate?
    VIII. If we should resolve upon going to Balmoral, which route would you recommend? Also name any "models" that may be known to you in that direction; stating landlady's name, and if married or single.

    We are, your admiring followers,

Henry John Macdonald.
A. F. Campbell.
S. Donald Stewart.21

ODE TO WILLIAM M'GONAGALL,

POET AND TRAGEDIAN, DUNDEE.

AMONG the poets of the present day
There is no one on earth who can possibly be able for to gainsay
But that William M'Gonagall' poet and tragedian,
Is truly the greatest poet that was ever found above or below the meridian.

'Twas in year '91, in the first month of spring,
On a very cold night, and the frost in full swing,
I met my friend Mactavish walking along the street,
And he gave me your "Poetic Gems" for to read them as a treat.

I took them home, and read them, and exclaimed,
Eureka! Eureka! M'Gonagall I proclaim
To have the deepest insight into human nature of any man I know,
As the reading of his "Gems" doth most emphatically show.

He reaches with poetic power the higher flights of song,
And like the eagle near the clouds, he soars serene and strong;
No common fowl is he, to roost on fence or crow about a barn,
He warbles sweet his wood-notes wild, and tell no common "yarn."

A better poet was never seen in the city of Dundee at any time,
And never again shall be, as far as I can see in the meantime:
His poem on the Tay Bridge is most beautiful to be read,
As I found by reading it one cold night before I went to bed.

Also his poem about the Emperor of Germany's funeral is the
    work of a master-mind,
And rivals in merit the greatest plays that the "Bard of Avon" left behind,
And it will be read when Milton's "Paradise Lost" is totally forgotten,
And all other poetic gems save those of William M'Gonagall are rotten.

But not till then will the world ever come to see
The wealth and beauty of the "Poetic Gems" of M'Gonagall'
    poet and tragedian, of Dundee;
And though his book can now be bought at the modest price of a shilling,
You can never get anywhere, at any price, a product quite so thrilling.

At the beginning of the volume is to be seen the classic head
Of the greatest tragedian that ever the boards did tread,
For to act the Thane of Fife, or discourse with spirits from beneath,
And cry in tones of thunder: "Command! they stand upon the heath."

Also his ode on the death of George Gilfillan
Shows that he was a true gentleman and no villain;
His poem on the funeral of the illustrious Prince Leopold

Would almost make any one weep for to behold.

Any one who would read his lines on Queen Victoria
Would never again be troubled with melancholia,
Because she has been a good Queen, and by no means bad,
Which, if she were, would indeed be sad.

And though she did not receive M'Gonagall at her castle of Balmoral,
The wreath that binds the poet's brow should be something more than floral,—
A wreath that will flourish evergreen in all the coming time,
When the name of the great M'Gonagall shall be known from clime to clime.

They will one day yet rear him monuments of brass, and weep upon his grave,
Though when he was living they would hardly have given him the price of a shave;
But his peerless, priceless "Poetic Gems" will settle once for all
The claim to immortality of William M'Gonagall.

TRIBUTE FROM ZULULAND.

The Royal Scots, Fort Curtis, Eokowe,
Zululand, 26th January 1891.

Poet M'Gonagall'—I received a copy of your poems recently from home, and take the first opportunity of congratulating you on the production of such a splendid work. Your poems show a taste not to be met with in many of the writings of the present age, and one can only wonder how you could have produced such a selection of poems, commencing as you did at such a late stage in life. I lent your book to a large number of my friends in the regiment who hail both from England and Scotland, and they one and all assert that it surpasses, in tone and clearness of expression, any of the writings of the so-called "poets" of the present day. I am confident your book would command an extraordinary sale if you arranged for its being sent out to the Cape or Natal Colonies, wherein so many well-known men reside who hail from the "land o' cakes." In Kimberley your work is extensively read and highly appreciated, but it is mainly obtained from friends at home, and not from local publishers. Trusting you may enjoy many years of excellent health, so as you can give us yet another proof of your poetical abilities, I remain, your sincere well-wisher.

FEED. ROLLO, 1st Royal Scots.

TESTIMONIALS.

We willingly certify that the bearer, Mr William M'Gonagall' has considerable ability in recitation. We have heard him recite some passages from Shakspeare with great force; and are of opinion that he is quite competent to read or recite passages from the poets and orators in villages and country towns with pleasure and profit to his audience. We also believe him to be a respectable man.

ISLAY BURNS, Minister of St. Peter's F. Church.
JOHN ALEX. BANKS, M.A. Edin., Headmaster,
   Propy. School, Dundee.
WILLIAM KNIGHT, Assistant, Free St. John's Ch.,
   Dundee (now Professor, St. Andrews Univ.).

29th March 1864.

Dundee, 30th May 1865.

I certify that William M'Gonagall has for some time been known to me. I have heard him speak, he has a strong proclivity for the elocutionary department, a strong voice, and great enthusiasm. He has had a good deal of experience too, having addressed audiences, and enacted parts here and elsewhere.

GEORGE GILFILLAN.

POETIC GEMS.

AN ODE TO THE QUEEN ON HER JUBILEE YEAR.

SOUND drums and trumpets, far and near!
And let all Queen Victoria's subjects loudly cheer!
And show by their actions that her they revere,
Because she's served them faithfully fifty long year!

All hail to the Empress of India and Great Britain's Queen!
Long may she live happy and serene!
And as this is now her Jubilee year,
I hope her subjects will show their loyalty without fear.

Therefore let all her subjects rejoice and sing,
Until they make the welkin ring;
And let young and old on this her Jubilee be glad,
And cry, "Long Live our Queen!" and don't be sad.

She has been a good Queen, which no one dare gainsay,
And I hope God will protect her for many a day;
May He enable her a few more years to reign,
And let all her lieges say—Amen!

Let all hatred towards her be thrown aside
All o'er her dominions broad and wide;
And let all her subjects bear in mind,
By God kings and queens are put in trust o'er mankind.

Therefore rejoice and be glad on her Jubilee day,
And try and make the heart of our Queen feel gay;
Oh! try and make her happy in country and town,
And not with Shakspeare say, "uneasy lies the head that wears a crown."

And as this is her first Jubilee year,
And will be her last, I rather fear;
Therefore, sound drums and trumpets cheerfully,
Until the echoes are heard o'er land and sea.

And let the innocent voices of the children at home or abroad
Ascend with cheerful shouts to the throne of God;
And sing aloud, "God Save our Gracious Queen!"
Because a good and charitable Sovereign she has been.

Therefore, ye sons of Great Britain, come join with me,
And welcome in our noble Queen's Jubilee;
Because she has been a faithful Queen, ye must confess,
There hasn't been her equal since the days of Queen Bess.

Therefore let all her lieges shout and cheer,
"God Save our Gracious Queen!" for many a year;
Let such be the cry in the peasant's cot, and hall,
With stentorian voices, as loud as they can bawl.

And let bonfires be kindled on every hill,
And her subjects dance around them at their freewill;
And try to drive dull care away
By singing and rejoicing on the Queen's Jubilee day.

May God protect her for many a day,
At home or abroad when she's far away;
Long may she be spared o'er her subjects to reign,
And let each and all with one voice say—Amen!

Victoria is a good Queen, which all her subjects know,
And for that may God protect her from every foe;
May He be as a hedge around her, as He's been all along,
And let her live and die in peace—is the end of my song.

THE DEATH OF PRINCE LEOPOLD.

ALAS! noble Prince Leopold, he is dead!
Who often has his lustre shed:
Especially by singing for the benefit of Esher School,—
Which proves he was a wise prince, and no conceited fool.

Methinks I see him on the platform singing the *Sands o' Dee*,
The generous-hearted Leopold, the good and the free,
Who was manly in his actions, and beloved by his mother;
And in all the family she hasn't got such another.

He was of a delicate constitution all his life,
And he was his mother's favourite, and very kind to his wife,
And he had also a particular liking for his child,
And in his behaviour he was very mild.

Oh! noble-hearted Leopold, most beautiful to see,
Who was wont to fill your audience's hearts with glee,
With your charming songs, and lectures against strong drink:
Britain had nothing else to fear, as far as you could think.

A wise prince you were, and well worthy of the name,
And to write in praise of thee I cannot refrain;
Because you were ever ready to defend that which is right,
Both pleasing and righteous in God's eye-sight.

And for the loss of such a prince the people will mourn,
But, alas! unto them he can never more return,
Because sorrow never could revive the dead again,
Therefore to weep for him is all in vain.

'Twas on Saturday the 12th of April, in the year 1884,
He was buried in the royal vault, never to rise more
Until the great and fearful judgment-day,
When the last trump shall sound to summon him away.

When the Duchess of Albany arrived she drove through the Royal Arch,—
A little before the Seaforth Highlanders set out on the funeral march;
And she was received with every sympathetic respect,
Which none of the people present seem'd to neglect.

Then she entered the memorial chapel and stayed a short time,
And as she viewed her husband's remains it was really sublime,
While her tears fell fast on the coffin lid without delay,
Then she took one last fond look, and hurried away.

At half-past ten o'clock the Seaforth Highlanders did appear,
And every man in the detachment his medals did wear;
And they carried their side-arms by their side,

With mournful looks, but full of love and pride.

Then came the Coldstream Guards headed by their band,
Which made the scene appear imposing and grand;
Then the musicians drew up in front of the guard-room,
And waited patiently to see the prince laid in the royal tomb.

First in the procession were the servants of His late Royal Highness,
And next came the servants of the Queen in deep mourning dress,
And the gentlemen of his household in deep distress,
Also General Du Pla, who accompanied the remains from Cannes.

The coffin was borne by eight Highlanders of his own regiment,
And the fellows seemed to be rather discontent
For the loss of the prince they loved most dear,
While adown their cheeks stole many a silent tear.

Then behind the corpse came the Prince of Wales in field-marshal uniform,
Looking very pale, dejected, careworn, and forlorn;
Then followed great magnates, all dressed in uniform,
And last, but not least, the noble Marquis of Lorne.

The scene in George's Chapel was most magnificent to behold,
The banners of the knights of the garter embroidered with gold;
Then again it was most touching and lovely to see
The Seaforth Highlanders' inscription to the Prince's memory:

It was wrought in violets, upon a background of white flowers,
And as they gazed upon it their tears fell in showers;
But the whole assembly were hushed when Her Majesty did appear,
Attired in her deepest mourning, and from her eye there fell a tear.

Her Majesty was unable to stand long, she was overcome with grief,
And when the Highlanders lowered the coffin into the tomb she felt relief;
Then the ceremony closed with singing "Lead, kindly light,"
Then the Queen withdrew in haste from the mournful sight.

Then the Seaforth Highlanders' band played "Lochaber no more,"
While the brave soldiers' hearts felt depressed and sore;
And as homeward they marched they let fall many a tear
For the loss of the virtuous Prince Leopold they loved so dear

THE DEATH OF LORD AND LADY DALHOUSIE.

ALAS! Lord and Lady Dalhousie are dead, and buried at last,
Which causes many people to feel a little downcast;
And both lie side by side in one grave,
But I hope God in His goodness their souls will save.

And may He protect their children that are left behind,
And may they always food and raiment find;
And from the paths of virtue may they ne'er be led,
And may they always find a house wherein to lay their head.

Lord Dalhousie was a man worthy of all praise,
And to his memory I hope a monument the people will raise,
That will stand for many ages to come
To commemorate the good deeds he has done.

He was beloved by men of high and low degree,
Especially in Forfarshire by his tenantry:
And by many of the inhabitants in and around Dundee.
Because he was affable in temper, and void of all vanity.

He had great affection for his children, also his wife,
'Tis said he loved her as dear as his life;
And I trust they are now in heaven above,
Where all is joy, peace, and love.

At the age of fourteen he resolved to go to sea,
So he entered the training-ship Britannia belonging the navy,
And entered as a midshipman as he considered most fit,
Then passed through the course of training with the greatest credit.

In a short time he obtained the rank of lieutenant,
Then to her Majesty's ship Galatea he was sent;
Which was under the command of the Duke of Edinburgh,
And during his service there he felt but little sorrow.

And from that he was promoted to be commander of the Britannia,
And was well liked by the men, for what he said was law;
And by him Prince Albert Victor and Prince George received a naval education,
Which met with the Prince of Wales' most hearty approbation.

'Twas in the year 1877 he married the Lady Ada Louisa Bennett,
And by marrying that noble lady he ne'er did regret;
And he was ever ready to give his service in any way,
Most willingly and cheerfully by night or by day.

'Twas in the year of 1887, and on Thursday the 1st of December,
Which his relatives and friends will long remember
That were present at the funeral in Cockpen churchyard,

Because they had for the noble Lord a great regard.

About eleven o'clock the remains reached Dalhousie,
And were met by a body of the tenantry;
They conveyed them inside the building, all seemingly woebegone,
And among those that sent wreaths was Lord Claude Hamilton.

Those that sent wreaths were but very few,
But one in particular was the Duke of Buccleuch;
Besides Dr. Herbert Spencer, and Countess Rosebery, and Lady Bennett,
Which no doubt were sent by them with heartfelt regret.

Besides those that sent wreaths in addition were the Earl and
    Countess of Aberdeen,
Especially the Prince of Wales' was most lovely to be seen,
And the Earl of Dalkeith's wreath was very pretty too,
With a mixture of green and white flowers, beautiful to view.

Amongst those present at the interment were Mr Marjori-banks, M.P.,
Also ex-Provost Ballingall from Bonnie Dundee;
Besides the Honourable W. G. Colville, representing the Duke
    and Duchess of Edinburgh,
While in every one's face standing at the grave was depicted sorrow.

The funeral service was conducted in the Church of Cockpen
By the Rev. J. Crabb, of St. Andrew's Episcopal Church, town of Brechin;
And as the two coffins were lowered into their last resting place,
Then the people retired with sad hearts at a quick pace.

THE FUNERAL OF THE GERMAN EMPEROR.

YE sons of Germany, your noble Emperor William now is dead,
Who oft great armies to battle hath led;
He was a man beloved by his subjects all,
Because he never tried them to enthral.

The people of Germany have cause now to mourn
The loss of their hero, who to them will ne'er return;
But his soul I hope to Heaven has fled away,
To the realms of endless bliss for ever and aye.

He was much respected throughout Europe by the high and the low,
And all over Germany people's hearts are full of woe;
For in the battlefield he was a hero bold,
Nevertheless, a lover of peace, to his credit be it told.

'Twas in the year of 1888, and on March the 16th day,
That the peaceful William's remains were conveyed away
To the royal mausoleum of Charlottenburg, their last resting-place,
The God-fearing man that never did his country disgrace.

The funeral service was conducted in the cathedral by the court
    chaplain, Dr. Kogel,
Which touched the hearts of his hearers, as from his lips it fell,
And in conclusion he recited the Lord's Prayer
In the presence of kings, princes, dukes, and counts assembled there.

And at the end of the service the infantry outside fired volley after volley,
While the people inside the cathedral felt melancholy,
As the sound of the musketry smote upon the ear,
In honour of the illustrious William, whom they loved most dear.

Then there was a solemn pause as the kings and princes took their places,
Whilst the hot tears are trickling down their faces,
And the mourners from shedding tears couldn't refrain;
And in respect of the good man, above the gateway glared a bituminous flame.

Then the coffin was placed on the funeral car,
By the kings and princes that came from afar;
And the Crown Prince William heads the procession alone,
While behind him are the four heirs-apparent to the throne.

Then followed the three Kings of Saxony, and the King of the Belgians also,
Together with the Prince of Wales, with their hearts full of woe,
Besides the Prince of Naples and Prince Rudolph of Austria were there,
Also the Czarevitch, and other princes in their order I do declare.

And as the procession passes the palace the blinds are drawn completely,
And every house is half hidden with the sable drapery;

And along the line of march expansive arches were erected,
While the spectators standing by seemed very dejected.

And through the Central Avenue, to make the decorations complete,
There were pedestals erected, rising fourteen to fifteen feet,
And at the foot and top of each pedestal were hung decorations of green bay,
Also beautiful wreaths and evergreen festoons all in grand array.

And there were torches fastened on pieces of wood stuck in the ground;
And as the people gazed on the wierd-like scene, their silence was profound;
And the shopkeepers closed their shops, and hotel-keepers closed
    in the doorways,
And with torchlight and gaslight, Berlin for once was all ablaze.

The authorities of Berlin in honour of the Emperor considered it no sin,
To decorate with crape the beautiful city of Berlin;
Therefore Berlin I declare was a city of crape,
Because few buildings crape decoration did escape.

First in the procession was the Emperor's bodyguard,
And his great love for them nothing could it retard;
Then followed a squadron of the hussars with their band,
Playing "Jesus, Thou my Comfort," most solemn and grand.

And to see the procession passing the sightseers tried their best,
Especially when the cavalry hove in sight, riding four abreast;
Men and officers with their swords drawn, a magnificent sight to see
In the dim sun's rays, their burnished swords glinting dimly.

Then followed the footguards with slow and solemn tread,
Playing the "Dead March in Saul," most appropriate for the dead;
And behind them followed the artillery, with four guns abreast,
Also the ministers and court officials dressed in their best.

The whole distance to the grave was covered over with laurel and bay,
So that the body should be borne along smoothly all the way;
And the thousands of banners in the procession were beautiful to view,
Because they were composed of cream-coloured silk and light blue.

There were thousands of thousands of men and women gathered there,
And standing ankle deep in snow, and seemingly didn't care
So as they got a glimpse of the funeral car,
Especially the poor souls that came from afar.

And when the funeral car appeared there was a general hush,
And the spectators in their anxiety to see began to crush;
And when they saw the funeral car by the Emperor's charger led,
Every hat and cap was lifted reverently from off each head.

And as the procession moved on to the royal mausoleum,
The spectators remained bareheaded and seemingly quite dumb;

And as the coffin was borne into its last resting-place,
Sorrow seemed depicted in each one's face.

And after the burial service the mourners took a last farewell
Of the noble-hearted William they loved so well;
Then rich and poor dispersed quietly that were assembled there,
While two batteries of field-guns fired a salute which did rend the air
In honour of the immortal hero they loved so dear,
The founder of the Fatherland, Germany, that he did revere.

THE BATTLE OF TEL-EL-KEBIR.

YE sons of Great Britain, come join with me,
And sing in praise of Sir Garnet Wolseley;
Sound drums and trumpets cheerfully,
For he has acted most heroically.

Therefore loudly his praises sing
Until the hills their echoes back doth ring;
For he is a noble hero bold,
And an honour to his Queen and country, be it told.

He has gained for himself fame and renown.
Which to posterity will be handed down;
Because he has defeated Arabi by land and by sea,
And from the battle of Tel-el-Kebir he made him to flee.

With an army about fourteen thousand strong,
Through Egypt he did fearlessly march along,
With the gallant and brave Highland brigade,
To whom honour is due, be it said.

Arabi's army was about seventy thousand in all,
And, virtually speaking, it wasn't very small;
But if they had been as numerous again,
The Irish and Highland brigades would have beaten them, it is plain.

'Twas on the 13th day of September, in the year of 1882,
Which Arabi and his rebel horde long will rue;
Because Sir Garnet Wolseley and his brave little band
Fought and conquered them on Kebir land.

He marched upon the enemy with his gallant band
O'er the wild and lonely desert sand,
And attacked them before daylight,
And in twenty minutes he put them to flight.

The first shock of the attack was borne by the Second Brigade,
Who behaved most manfully, it is said,
Under the command of brave General Grahame,
And have gained a lasting honour to their name.

But Major Hart and the 18th Royal Irish, conjoint,
Carried the trenches at the bayonet's point;
Then the Marines chased them about four miles away,
At the charge of the bayonet, without dismay!

General Sir Archibald Alison led on the Highland Brigade,
Who never were the least afraid.
And such has been the case in this Egyptian war,

For at the charge of the bayonet they ran from them afar!

With their bagpipes playing, and one ringing cheer,
And the 42nd soon did the trenches clear;
Then hand to hand they did engage,
And fought like tigers in a cage.

Oh! it must have been a glorious sight
To see Sir Garnet Wolseley in the thickest of the fight!
In the midst of shot and shell, and the cannon's roar,
Whilst the dead and the dying lay weltering in their gore.

Then the Egyptians were forced to yield,
And the British were left masters of the field;
Then Arabi he did fret and frown
To see his army thus cut down.

Then Arabi the rebel took to flight,
And spurred his Arab steed with all his might:
With his heart full of despair and woe,
And never halted till he reached Cairo.

Now since the Egyptian war is at an end,
Let us thank God! Who did send
Sir Garnet Wolseley to crush and kill
Arabi and his rebel army at Kebir hill.

THE FAMOUS TAY WHALE.

'TWAS In the month of December, and in the year 1883,
That a monster whale came to Dundee,
Resolved for a few days to sport and play,
And devour the small fishes in the silvery Tay.

So the monster whale did sport and play
Among the innocent little fishes in the beautiful Tay,
Until he was seen by some men one day,
And they resolved to catch him without delay.

When it came to be known a whale was seen in the Tay,
Some men began to talk and to say,
We must try and catch this monster of a whale,
So come on, brave boys, and never say fail.

Then the people together in crowds did run,
Resolved to capture the whale and to have some fun!
So small boats were launched on the silvery Tay,
While the monster of the deep did sport and play.

Oh! it was a most fearful and beautiful sight,
To see it lashing the water with its tail all its might,
And making the water ascend like a shower of hail,
With one lash of its ugly and mighty tail.

Then the water did descend on the men in the boats,
Which wet their trousers and also their coats;
But it only made them the more determined to catch the whale,
But the whale shook at them his tail.

Then the whale began to puff and to blow,
While the men and the boats after him did go,
Armed well with harpoons for the fray,
Which they fired at him without dismay.

And they laughed and grinned just like wild baboons,
While they fired at him their sharp harpoons:
But when struck with the harpoons he dived below,
Which filled his pursuers' hearts with woe:

Because they guessed they had lost a prize,
Which caused the tears to well up in their eyes;
And in that their anticipations were only right,
Because he sped on to Stonehaven with all his might:

And was first seen by the crew of a Gourdon fishing boat,
Which they thought was a big coble upturned afloat;
But when they drew near they saw it was a whale,
So they resolved to tow it ashore without fail.

So they got a rope from each boat tied round his tail,
And landed their burden at Stonehaven without fail;
And when the people saw it their voices they did raise,
Declaring that the brave fishermen deserved great praise.

And my opinion is that God sent the whale in time of need,
No matter what other people may think or what is their creed;
I know fishermen in general are often very poor,
And God in His goodness sent it to drive poverty from their door.

So Mr John Wood has bought it for two hundred and twenty-six pound,
And has brought it to Dundee all safe and all sound;
Which measures 40 feet in length from the snout to the tail,
So I advise the people far and near to see it without fail.

Then hurrah! for the mighty monster whale,
Which has got 17 feet 4 inches from tip to tip of a tail!
Which can be seen for a sixpence or a shilling,
That is to say, if the people all are willing.

THE RAILWAY BRIDGE OF THE SILVERY TAY.

BEAUTIFUL Railway Bridge of the Silvery Tay!
With your numerous arches and pillars in so grand array,
And your central girders, which seem to the eye
To be almost towering to the sky.
The greatest wonder of the day,
And a great beautification to the River Tay,
Most beautiful to be seen,
Near by Dundee and the Magdalen Green.

Beautiful Railway Bridge of the Silvery Tay!
That has caused the Emperor of Brazil to leave
His home far away, *incognito* in his dress,
And view thee ere he passed along *en route* to Inverness.

Beautiful Railway Bridge of the Silvery Tay!
The longest of the present day
That has ever crossed o'er a tidal river stream,
Most gigantic to be seen,
Near by Dundee and the Magdalen Green.

Beautiful Railway Bridge of the Silvery Tay!
Which will cause great rejoicing on the opening day,
And hundreds of people will come from far away,
Also the Queen, most gorgeous to be seen,
Near by Dundee and the Magdalen Green.

Beautiful Railway Bridge of the Silvery Tay!
And prosperity to Provost Cox, who has given
Thirty thousand pounds and upwards away
In helping to erect the Bridge of the Tay,
Most handsome to be seen,
Near by Dundee and the Magdalen Green.

Beautiful Railway Bridge of the Silvery Tay!
I hope that God will protect all passengers
By night and by day,
And that no accident will befall them while crossing
The Bridge of the Silvery Tay,
For that would be most awful to be seen
Near by Dundee and the Magdalen Green.

Beautiful Railway Bridge of the Silvery Tay!
And prosperity to Messrs Bouche and Grothe,
The famous engineers of the present day,
Who have succeeded in erecting the Railway
Bridge of the Silvery Tay,
Which stands unequalled to be seen
Near by Dundee and the Magdalen Green.

THE NEWPORT RAILWAY.

SUCCESS to the Newport Railway,
Along the braes of the Silvery Tay,
And to Dundee straightway,
Across the Railway Bridge o' the Silvery Tay,
Which was opened on the 12th of May,
In the year of our Lord 1879,
Which will clear all expenses in a very short time
Because the thrifty housewives of Newport
To Dundee will often resort,
Which will be to them profit and sport,
By bringing cheap tea, bread, and jam,
And also some of Lipton's ham,
Which will make their hearts feel light and gay,
And cause them to bless the opening day
Of the Newport Railway.
The train is most beautiful to be seen,
With its long, white curling cloud of steam,
As the train passes on her way
Along the bonnie braes o' the Silvery Tay.

And if the people of Dundee
Should feel inclined to have a spree,
I am sure 'twill fill their hearts with glee
By crossing o'er to Newport,
And there they can have excellent sport,
By viewing the scenery beautiful and gay,
During the livelong summer day,

And then they can return at night
With spirits light and gay,
By the Newport Railway,
By night or by day,
Across the Railway Bridge o' the Silvery Tay.

Success to the undertakers of the Newport Railway,
Hoping the Lord will their labours repay,
And prove a blessing to the people
For many a long day
Who live near by Newport,
On the bonnie braes o' the Silvery Tay.

THE TAY BRIDGE DISASTER.

Beautiful Railway Bridge of the Silv'ry Tay!
Alas! I am very sorry to say
That ninety lives have been taken away
On the last Sabbath day of 1879,
Which will be remember'd for a very long time.

Twas about seven o'clock at night,
And the wind it blew with all its might,
And the rain came pouring down,
And the dark clouds seem'd to frown,
And the Demon of the air seem'd to say—
"I'll blow down the Bridge of Tay."

When the train left Edinburgh
The passengers' hearts were light and felt no sorrow,
But Boreas blew a terrific gale,
Which made their hearts for to quail,
And many of the passengers with fear did say—
"I hope God will send us safe across the Bridge of Tay."

But when the train came near to Wormit Bay,
Boreas he did loud and angry bray,
And shook the central girders of the Bridge of Tay
On the last Sabbath day of 1879,
Which will be remember'd for a very long time.

So the train sped on with all its might,
And Bonnie Dundee soon hove in sight,
And the passengers' hearts felt light,
Thinking they would enjoy themselves on the New Year,
With their friends at home they lov'd most dear,
And wish them all a happy New Year.

So the train mov'd slowly along the Bridge of Tay,
Until it was about midway,
Then the central girders with a crash gave way,
And down went the train and passengers into the Tay!
The Storm Fiend did loudly bray,
Because ninety lives had been taken away,
On the last Sabbath day of 1879,
Which will be remember'd for a very long time.

As soon as the catastrophe came to be known
The alarm from mouth to mouth was blown,
And the cry rang out all o'er the town,
Good Heavens! the Tay Bridge is blown down,

And a passenger train from Edinburgh,
Which fill'd all the people's hearts with sorrow,
And made them for to turn pale,
Because none of the passengers were sav'd to tell the tale
How the disaster happen'd on the last Sabbath day of 1879,
Which will be remember'd for a very long time.

It must have been an awful sight,
To witness in the dusky moonlight,
While the Storm Fiend did laugh, and angry did bray,
Along the Railway Bridge of the Silv'ry Tay.
Oh! ill-fated Bridge of the Silv'ry Tay,
I must now conclude my lay
By telling the world fearlessly without the least dismay.
That your central girders would not have given way,
At least many sensible men do say,
Had they been supported on each side with buttresses,
At least many sensible men confesses,
For the stronger we our houses do build,
The less chance we have of being killed.

AN ADDRESS TO THE NEW TAY BRIDGE.

BEAUTIFUL new railway bridge of the Silvery Tay,
With your strong brick piers and buttresses in so grand array,
And your thirteen central girders, which seem to my eye
Strong enough all windy storms to defy.
And as I gaze upon thee my heart feels gay,
Because thou are the greatest railway bridge of the present day,
And can be seen for miles away
From north, south, east, or west of the Tay
On a beautiful and clear sunshiny day,
And ought to make the hearts of the "Mars" boys feel gay,
Because thine equal nowhere can be seen,
Only near by Dundee and the bonnie Magdalen Green.

Beautiful new railway bridge of the Silvery Tay,
With thy beautiful side-screens along your railway,
Which will be a great protection on a windy day,
So as the railway carriages won't be blown away,
And ought to cheer the hearts of the passengers night and day
As they are conveyed along thy beautiful railway,
And towering above the silvery Tay,
Spanning the beautiful river shore to shore
Upwards of two miles and more,
Which is most wonderful to be seen
Near by Dundee and the bonnie Magdalen Green.

Thy structure to my eye seems strong and grand,
And the workmanship most skilfully planned;
And I hope the designers, Messrs Barlow & Arrol, will prosper for many a day
For erecting thee across the beautiful Tay.
And I think nobody need have the least dismay
To cross o'er thee by night or by day,
Because thy strength is visible to be seen
Near by Dundee and the bonnie Magdalen Green.

Beautiful new railway bridge of the Silvery Tay,
I wish you success for many a year and a day,
And I hope thousands of people will come from far away,
Both high and low without delay,
From the north, south, east, and the west,
Because as a railway bridge thou are the best;
Thou standest unequalled to be seen
Near by Dundee and the bonnie Magdalen Green.

And for beauty thou art most lovely to be seen
As the train crosses o'er thee with her cloud of steam;

And you look well, painted the colour of marone,
And to find thy equal there is none,
Which, without fear of contradiction, I venture to say,
Because you are the longest railway bridge of the present day
That now crosses o'er a tidal river stream,
And the most handsome to be seen
Near by Dundee and the bonnie Magdalen Green.

The New Yorkers boast about their Brooklyn Bridge,
But in comparison to thee it seems like a midge,
Because thou spannest the silvery Tay
A mile and more longer I venture to say;
Besides the railway carriages are pulled across by a rope,
Therefore Brooklyn Bridge cannot with thee cope;
And as you have been opened on the 20th day of June,
I hope Her Majesty Queen Victoria will visit thee very soon,
Because thou are worthy of a visit from Duke, Lord, or Queen,
And strong and securely built, which is most worthy to be seen
Near by Dundee and the bonnie Magdalen Green.

THE LATE SIR JOHN OGILVY.

ALAS! Sir John Ogilvy is dead, aged eighty-seven,
But I hope his soul is now in heaven;
For he was a generous-hearted gentleman I am sure,
And, in particular, very kind unto the poor.

He was a Christian gentleman in every degree,
And, for many years, was an M.P. for Bonnie Dundee,
And, while he was an M.P., he didn't neglect
To advocate the rights of Dundee in every respect.

He was a public benefactor in many ways,
Especially in erecting an asylum for imbecile children to spend their days;
Then he handed the institution over as free,—
As a free gift and a boon to the people of Dundee.

He was chairman of several of the public boards in Dundee,
And among these were the Asylum Board and the Royal Infirmary;
In every respect he was a God-fearing true gentleman,
And to gainsay it there's nobody can.

He lived as a Christian gentleman in his time,
And he now lies buried in the family vault in Strathmartine;
But I hope his soul has gone aloft where all troubles cease,
Amongst the blessed saints where all is joy and peace.

To the people around Baldovan he will be a great loss,
Because he was a kind-hearted man and a Soldier of the Cross.
He had always a kind word for every one he met,
And the loss of such a good man will be felt with deep regret.

Because such men as Sir John Ogilvy are hard to be found,
Especially in Christian charity his large heart did abound,
Therefore a monument should be erected for him most handsome to behold,
And his good deeds engraven thereon in letters of gold.

THE RATTLING BOY FROM DUBLIN.

I'M a rattling boy from Dublin town,
I courted a girl called Biddy Brown,
Her eyes they were as black as sloes,
She had black hair and an aquiline nose.

Chorus—
    Whack fal de da, fal de darelido,
    Whack fal de da, fal de darelay,
    Whack fal de da, fal de darelido,
    Whack fal de da, fal de darelay.

One night I met her with another lad,
Says I, Biddy, I've caught you, by dad;
I never thought you were half so bad
As to be going about with another lad.
    Chorus.

Says I, Biddy, this will never do,
For to-night you've prov'd to me untrue,
So do not make a hullaballoo,
For I will bid farewell to you.
    Chorus.

Says Barney Magee, She is my lass,
And the man that says no, he is an ass,
So come away, and I'll give you a glass,
Och, sure you can get another lass.
    Chorus.

Says I, To the devil with your glass,
You have taken from me my darling lass,
And if you look angry, or offer to frown.
With my darling shillelah I'll knock you down.
    Chorus.

Says Barney Magee unto me,
By the hokey I love Biddy Brown,
And before I'll give her up to thee,
One or both of us will go down.
    Chorus.

So, with my darling shillelah, I gave him a whack,
Which left him lying on his back,
Saying, botheration to you and Biddy Brown,—
For I'm the rattling boy from Dublin town.
    Chorus.

So a policeman chanced to come up at the time,
And he asked of me the cause of the shine,
Says I, he threatened to knock me down
When I challenged him for walking with my Biddy Brown.
    Chorus.

So the policeman took Barney Magee to jail,
Which made him shout and bewail
That ever he met with Biddy Brown,
The greatest deceiver in Dublin town.
    Chorus.

So I bade farewell to Biddy Brown,
The greatest jilter in Dublin town,
Because she proved untrue to me,
And was going about with Barney Magee.
    Chorus.

THE BURIAL OF THE REV. GEORGE GILFILLAN.

ON the Gilfillan burial day,
In the Hill o' Balgay,
It was a most solemn sight to see,
Not fewer than thirty thousand people assembled in Dundee,
All watching the funeral procession of "Gilfillan that day,
That death had suddenly taken away,
And was going to be buried in the Hill o' Balgay.

There were about three thousand people in the procession alone,
And many were shedding tears, and several did moan,
And their bosoms heaved with pain,
Because they knew they would never look upon his like again.

There could not be fewer than fifty carriages in the procession hat day,
And gentlemen in some of them that had come from far away,
And in whispers some of them did say,
As the hearse bore the precious corpse away,
Along the Nethergate that day.
I'm sure he will be greatly missed by the poor,
For he never turned them empty-handed away from his door;
And to assist them in distress it didn't give him pain,
And I'm sure the poor will never look upon his like again.

On the Gilfillan burial day, in the Hill o' Balgay,
There was a body of policemen marshalled in grand array,
And marched in front of the procession all the way;
Also the relatives and friends of the deceas'd,
Whom I hope from all sorrows has been releas'd,
And whose soul I hope to heaven has fled away,
To sing with saints above for ever and aye.

The Provost, Magistrates, and Town Council were in the procession that day;
Also Mrs Gilfillan, who cried and sobbed all the way
For her kind husband, that was always affable and gay,
Which she will remember until her dying day.

When the procession arrived in the Hill o' Balgay,
The people were almost as hush as death, and many of them did say—
As long as we live we'll remember the day
That the great Gilfillan was buried in the Hill o' Balgay.

When the body of the great Gilfillan was lowered into the grave,
'Twas then the people's hearts with sorrow did heave;
And with tearful eyes and bated breath,
Mrs Gilfillan lamented her loving husband's death.

Then she dropped a ringlet of immortelles into his grave,
Then took one last fond look, and in sorrow did leave;
And all the people left with sad hearts that day,
And that ended the Gilfillan burial in the Hill o' Balgay.

THE BATTLE OF EL-TEB.

YE sons of Great Britain, I think no shame
To write in praise of brave General Graham!
Whose name will be handed down to posterity without any stigma,
Because, at the battle of El-Teb, he defeated Osman Digna.

With an army about five thousand strong,
To El-Teb, in the year 1884, he marched along,
And bivouacked there for the night;
While around their fires they only thought of the coming fight.

They kept up their fires all the long night,
Which made the encampment appear weird-like to the sight;
While the men were completely soaked with the rain,
But the brave heroes disdained to complain.

The brave heroes were glad when daylight did appear,
And when the reveille was sounded, they gave a hearty cheer
And their fires were piled up higher again,
Then they tried to dry their clothes that were soaked with the rain.

Then breakfast was taken about eight o'clock,
And when over, each man stood in the ranks as firm as a rock,
And every man seemed to be on his guard—
All silent and ready to move forward.

The first movement was a short one from where they lay—
Then they began to advance towards El-Teb without dismay,
And showed that all was in order for the fray,
While every man's heart seemed to feel light and gay.

The enemy's position could be seen in the distance far away
But the brave heroes marched on without delay—
Whilst the enemy's banners floated in the air,
And dark swarms of men were scattered near by there.

Their force was a large one—its front extended over a mile,
And all along the line their guns were all in file;
But, as the British advanced, they disappeared,
While our brave kilty lads loudly cheered.

Thus slowly and cautiously brave General Graham proceeded,
And to save his men from slaughter, great caution was needed,
Because Osman Digna's force was about ten thousand strong;
But he said, Come on, my brave lads, we'll conquer them ere long!

It was about ten o'clock when they came near the enemy's lines,
And on the morning air could be heard the cheerful chimes
Coming from the pipes of the gallant Black Watch,
Which every ear in the British force was eager to catch.

Then they passed by the enemy about mid-day,
While every Arab seemed to have his gun ready for the fray;
When a bullet strikes down General Baker by the way,
But he is soon in the saddle again without delay,

And ready for any service that he could perform;
Whilst the bullets fell around them in a perfect storm
That they had to lie down, but not through fear,
Because the enemy was about 800 yards on their left rear

Then General Graham addressed his men,
And said, If they won't attack us, we must attack them,
So start to your feet my lads, and never fear,
And strike up your bagpipes, and give a loud cheer.

So they leapt to their feet, and gave a loud cheer,
While the Arabs swept down upon them without the least fear,
And put aside their rifles, and grasped their spears;
Whilst the British bullets in front of them the earth uptears.

Then the British charged them with their cold steel,
Which made the Arabs backward for to reel;
But they dashed forward again on their ranks without dismay,
But before the terrible fire of their musketry they were swept away.

Oh, God of Heaven! it was a terrible sight
To see, and hear the Arabs shouting with all their might
A fearful oath when they got an inch of cold steel,
Which forced them backwards again, and made them reel.

By two o'clock they were fairly beat,
And Osman Digna, the false prophet, was forced to retreat
After three hours of an incessant fight;
But Heaven, 'tis said, defends the right.

And I think he ought to be ashamed of himself;
For I consider he has acted the part of a silly elf,
By thinking to conquer the armies of the Lord
With his foolish and benighted rebel horde.

THE BATTLE OE ABU KLEA.

YE sons of Mars, come join with me,
And sing in praise of Sir Herbert Stewart's little army,
That made ten thousand Arabs flee
At the charge of the bayonet at Abu Klea.

General Stewart's force was about fifteen hundred all told,
A brave little band, but, like lions bold,
They fought under their brave and heroic commander,
As gallant and as skilful as the great Alexander.

And the nation has every reason to be proud,
And in praise of his little band we cannot speak too loud,
Because that gallant fifteen hundred soon put to flight
Ten thousand Arabs, which was a most beautiful sight.

The enemy kept up a harmless fire all night,
And threw up works on General Stewart's right;
Therefore he tried to draw the enemy on to attack,
But they hesitated, and through fear drew back.

But General Stewart ordered his men forward in square,
All of them on foot, ready to die and to dare;
And he forced the enemy to engage in the fray,
But in a short time they were glad to run away.

But not before they penetrated through the British square,
Which was a critical moment to the British, I declare,
Owing to the great number of the Arabs,
Who rushed against their bayonets and received fearful stabs.

Then all was quiet again until after breakfast,
And when the brave little band had finished their repast,
Then the firing began from the heights on the right,
From the breastworks they had constructed during the night.

By eight o'clock the enemy was of considerable strength,
With their banners waving beautifully and of great length,
And creeping steadily up the grassy road direct to the wells,
But the British soon checked their advance by shot and shells.

At ten o'clock brave General Stewart made a counter-attack,
Resolved to turn the enemy on a different track;
And he ordered his men to form a hollow square,
Placing the Guards in the front, and telling them to prepare.

And on the left was the Mounted Infantry,
Which truly was a magnificent sight to see;
Then the Sussex Regiment was on the right,
And the Heavy Cavalry and Naval Brigade all ready to fight.

Then General Stewart took up a good position on a slope,
Where he guessed the enemy could not with him cope,
Where he knew the rebels must advance,
All up hill and upon open ground, which was his only chance.

Then Captain Norton's battery planted shells amongst the densest mass,
Determined with shot and shell the enemy to harass;
Then came the shock of the rebels against the British square,
While the fiendish shouts of the Arabs did rend the air.

But the steadiness of the Guards, Marines, and Infantry prevailed,
And for the loss of their brother officers they sadly bewailed,
Who fell mortally wounded in the bloody fray,
Which they will remember for many a long day.

For ten minutes a desperate struggle raged from left to rear,
While Gunner Smith saved Lieutenant Guthrie's life without dread or fear;
When all the other gunners had been borne back,
He took up a handspike, and the Arabs he did whack.

The noble hero hard blows did strike,
As he swung round his head the handspike;
He seemed like a destroying angel in the midst of the fight,
The way be scattered the Arabs left and right.

Oh! it was an exciting and terrible sight,
To see Colonel Burnaby engaged in the fight:
With sword in hand, fighting with might and main,
Until killed by a spear-thrust in the jugular vein.

A braver soldier ne'er fought on a battle-field,
Death or glory was his motto, rather than yield;
A man of noble stature and manly to behold,
And an honour to his country be it told.

It was not long before every Arab in the square was killed,
And with a dense smoke and dust the air was filled;
General Stewart's horse was shot, and he fell to the ground,
In the midst of shot and shell on every side around.

And when the victory was won they gave three British cheers,
While adown their cheeks flowed many tears
For their fallen comrades that lay weltering in their gore:
Then the square was re-formed, and the battle was o'er.

A CHRISTMAS CAROL.

WELCOME, sweet Christmas, blest be the morn
That Christ our Saviour was born!
Earth's Redeemer, to save us from all danger,
And, as the Holy Record tells, born in a manger.

   Chorus—Then ring, ring, Christmas bells,
        Till your sweet music o'er the kingdom swells
        To warn the people to respect the morn
        That Christ their Saviour was born.

The snow was on the ground when Christ was born,
And the Virgin Mary His mother felt very forlorn
As she lay in a horse's stall at a roadside inn,
Till Christ our Saviour was born to free us from sin.

Oh! think of the Virgin Mary as she lay
In a lowly stable on a bed of hay,
And angels watching o'er her till Christ was born,
Therefore all the people should respect Christmas morn

The way to respect Christmas time
Is not by drinking whisky or wine,
But to sing praises to God on Christmas morn,
The time that Jesus Christ His Son was born;

Whom He sent into the world to save sinners from hell,
And by believing in Him in heaven we'll dwell;
Then blest be the morn that Christ was born,
Who can save us from hell, death, and scorn.

Then be warned, and respect the Saviour dear,
And treat with less respect the New Year,
And respect always the blessed morn
That Christ our Saviour was born.

For each new morn to the Christian is dear,
As well as the morn of the New Year,
And he thanks God for the light of each new morn,
Especially the morn that Christ was born.

Therefore, good people, be warned in time,
And on Christmas morn don't get drunk with wine,
But praise God above on Christmas morn,
Who sent His Son to save us from hell and scorn.

There the heavenly babe He lay
In a stall among a lot of hay,
While the Angel Host by Bethlehem
Sang a beautiful and heavenly anthem.

Christmas time ought to be held most dear,
Much more so than the New Year,
Because that's the time that Christ was born,
Therefore respect Christmas morn.

And let the rich be kind to the poor,
And think of the hardships they do endure,
Who are neither clothed nor fed,
And many without a blanket to their bed.

THE CHRISTMAS GOOSE.

MR SMIGGS was a gentleman,
    And lived in London town;
His wife she was a good kind soul,
    And seldom known to frown.

'Twas on Christmas eve,
    And Smiggs and his wife lay cosy in bed,
When the thought of buying a goose
    Came into his head.

So the next morning,
    Just as the sun rose,
He jump'd out of bed,
    And he donn'd his clothes,

Saying, "Peggy, my dear,
    You need not frown,
For I'll buy you the best goose
    In all London town."

So away to the poultry shop he goes,
    And bought the goose, as he did propose,
And for it he paid one crown,
    The finest, he thought, in London town.

When Smiggs bought the goose
    He suspected no harm,
But a naughty boy stole it
    From under his arm.

Then Smiggs he cried, "Stop, thief!
    Come back with my goose!"
But the naughty boy laugh'd at him,
    And gave him much abuse.

But a policeman captur'd the naughty boy,
    And gave the goose to Smiggs,
And said he was greatly bother'd
    By a set of juvenile prigs.

So the naughty boy was put in prison
    For stealing the goose,
And got ten days' confinement
    Before he got loose.

So Smiggs ran home to his dear Peggy,
    Saying, "Hurry, and get this fat goose ready,
That I have bought for one crown;
    So, my darling, you need not frown."

"Dear Mr Smiggs, I will not frown:
    I'm sure 'tis cheap for one crown,
Especially at Christmas time—
    Oh! Mr Smiggs, it's really fine."

"Peggy, it is Christmas time,
    So let us drive dull care away,
For we have got a Christmas goose,
    So cook it well, I pray.

"No matter how the poor are clothed,
    Or if they starve at home,
We'll drink our wine, and eat our goose,
    Aye, and pick it to the bone."

AN AUTUMN REVERIE

Alas! beautiful Summer now hath fled,
And the face of Nature doth seem dead,
And the leaves are withered, and falling off the trees,
By the nipping and chilling autumnal breeze.

The pleasures of the little birds are all fled,
And with the cold many of them will be found dead,
Because the leaves of the trees are scattered in the blast,
And makes the feathered creatures feel downcast.

Because there are no leaves on the trees to shield them from the storm
On a windy, and rainy, cloudy morn;
Which makes their little hearts throb with pain,
By the chilling blast and the pitiless rain.

But still they are more contented than the children of God,
As long as they can pick up a worm from the sod,
Or anything they can get to eat,
Just, for instance, a stale crust of bread or a grain of wheat.

Oh! think of the little birds in the time of snow,
Also of the little street waifs, that are driven to and fro,
And trembling in the cold blast, and chilled to the bone,
For the want of food and clothing, and a warm home.

Besides think of the sorrows of the wandering poor,
That are wandering in the cold blast from door to door;
And begging, for Heaven's sake, a crust of bread,
And alas! not knowing where to lay their head.

While the rich are well fed and covered from the cold,
While the poor are starving, both young and old;
Alas! it is the case in this boasted Christian land,
Whereas the rich are told to be kind to the poor, is God's command.

Oh! think of the working man when he's no work to do,
Who's got a wife and family, perhaps four or two,
And the father searching for work, and no work can be had,
The thought, I'm sure, 'tis enough to drive the poor man mad.

Because for his wife and family he must feel,
And perhaps the thought thereof will cause him to steal
Bread for his family, that are starving at home,
While the thought thereof makes him sigh heavily and groan.

Alas! the pangs of hunger are very hard to thole,
And few people can their temper control,
Or become reconciled to their fate,
Especially when they cannot find anything to eat.

Oh! think of the struggles of the poor to make a living,
Because the rich unto them seldom are giving;
Whereas they are told he that giveth to the poor lendeth unto the Lord,
But alas! they rather incline their money to hoard.

Then there's the little news-vendors in the street,
Running about perhaps with bare feet;
And if the rich chance to see such creatures in the street,
In general they make a sudden retreat.

THE WRECK OF THE STEAMER "LONDON"
WHILE ON HER WAY TO AUSTRALIA.

'TWAS In the year of 1866, and on a very beautiful day,
That eighty-two passengers, with spirits light and gay,
Left Gravesend harbour, and sailed gaily away
On board the steamship "London,"
Bound for the city of Melbourne,
Which unfortunately was her last run,
Because she was wrecked on the stormy main,
Which has caused many a heart to throb with pain,
Because they will ne'er look upon their lost ones again.

'Twas on the 11th of January they anchored at the Nore;
The weather was charming—the like was seldom seen before,
Especially the next morning as they came in sight
Of the charming and beautiful Isle of Wight,
But the wind it blew a terrific gale towards night,
Which caused the passengers' hearts to shake with fright,
And caused many of them to sigh and mourn,
And whisper to themselves, We will ne'er see Melbourne.

Amongst the passengers was Gustavus V. Brooke,
Who was to be seen walking on the poop,
Also clergymen, and bankers, and magistrates also,
All chatting merrily together in the cabin below;
And also wealthy families returning to their dear native land.
And accomplished young ladies, most lovely and grand,
All in the beauty and bloom of their pride,
And some with their husbands sitting close by their side.

'Twas all on a sudden the storm did arise,
Which took the captain and passengers all by surprise,
Because they had just sat down to their tea,
When the ship began to roll with the heaving of the sea,
And shipped a deal of water, which came down on their heads,
Which wet their clothes and also their beds;
And caused a fearful scene of consternation,
And amongst the ladies great tribulation,
And made them cry out, Lord, save us from being drowned,
And for a few minutes the silence was profound.

Then the passengers began to run to and fro,
With buckets to bale out the water between decks below,
And Gustavus Brooke quickly leapt from his bed
In his Garibaldi jacket and drawers, without fear or dread,
And rushed to the pump, and wrought with might and main;

But alas! all their struggling was in vain,
For the water fast did on them gain;
But he enacted a tragic part until the last,
And sank exhausted when all succour was past;
While the big billows did lash her o'er,
And the Storm-fiend did laugh and roar.

Oh, Heaven! it must have really been
A most harrowing and pitiful scene
To hear mothers and their children loudly screaming,
And to see the tears adown their pale faces streaming,
And to see a clergyman engaged in prayer,
Imploring God their lives to spare, ...
Whilst the cries of the women and children did rend the air.

Then the captain cried, Lower down the small boats,
And see if either of them sinks or floats;
Then the small boats were launched on the stormy wave,
And each one tried hard his life to save
From a merciless watery grave . . . . .

A beautiful young lady did madly cry and rave,
"Five hundred sovereigns, my life to save!"
But she was by the sailors plainly told
For to keep her filthy gold, ...
Because they were afraid to overload the boat,
Therefore she might either sink or float,
Then she cast her eyes to Heaven, and cried, Lord, save me,
Then went down with the ship to the bottom of the sea,
Along with Gustavus Brooke, who was wont to fill our hearts with glee
While performing Shakespearian tragedy.

And out of eighty-two passengers only twenty were saved,
And that twenty survivors most heroically behaved.
For three stormy days and stormy nights they were tossed to and fro
On the raging billows, with their hearts full of woe,
Alas! poor souls, not knowing where to go,
Until at last they all agreed to steer for the south,
And they chanced to meet an Italian barque bound for Falmouth,
And they were all rescued from a watery grave,
And they thanked God and Captain Cavassa, who did their lives save.

THE WREAK OF THE "THOMAS DRYDEN" IN PENTLAND FIRTH.

As I stood upon the sandy beach
    One morn near Pentland Ferry,
I saw a beautiful brigantine,
    And all her crew seem'd merry.

When lo! the wind began to howl,
    And the clouds began to frown,
And in the twinkling of an eye
The rain came pouring down.

Then the sea began to swell,
    And seem'd like mountains high,
And the sailors on board that brigantine
    To God for help did loudly cry.

Oh! it was an awful sight
    To see them struggling with all their might,
And imploring God their lives to save
    From a merciless watery grave.

Their cargo consisted of window-glass,
    Also coal and linseed-oil,
Which helped to calm the raging sea
    That loud and angry did boil.

Because when the bottoms of the barrels
    Were with the raging billows stove in,
The oil spread o'er the water,
    And smoothed the stormy billows' din!

Then she began to duck in the trough of the sea,
    Which was fearful to behold;
And her crossyards dipped in the big billows
    As from side to side she rolled.

She was tossed about on the merciless sea,
    And received some terrible shocks,
Until at last she ran against
    A jagged reef of rocks.

'Twas then she was rent asunder,
    And the water did rush in—
It was most dreadful to hear it,
    It made such a terrific din.

Then the crew jumped into the small boats
    While the Storm-fiend did roar,
And were very near being drowned
    Before they got ashore.

Then the coal-dust blackened the water
    Around her where she lay,
And the barrels of linseed-oil
    They floated far away.

And when the crew did get ashore,
    They were shaking with cold and fright,
And they went away to Huna inn,
    And got lodgings for the night!

ATTEMPTED ASSASSINATION OF THE QUEEN.

GOD prosper long our noble Queen,
    And long may she reign!
Maclean he tried to shoot her,
    But it was all in vain.

For God He turned the ball aside
    Maclean aimed at her head;
And he felt very angry
    Because he didn't shoot her dead.

There's a divinity that hedgeth a king,
    And so it does seem,
And my opinion is, it has hedged
    Our most gracious Queen.

Maclean must be a madman,
    Which is obvious to be seen,
Or else he wouldn't have tried to shoot
    Our most beloved Queen.

Victoria is a good Queen,
    Which all her subjects know,
And for that God has protected her
    From all her deadly foes.

She is noble and generous,
    Her subjects must confess;
There hasn't been her equal
    Since the days of good Queen Bess.

Long may she be spared to roam
    Among the bonnie Highland floral,
And spend many a happy day
    In the palace of Balmoral.

Because she is very kind
    To the old women there,
And allows them bread, tea, and sugar,
    And each one to get a share.

And when they know of her coming,
    Their hearts feel overjoy'd,
Because, in general, she finds work
    For men that's unemploy'd.

And she also gives the gipsies money
    While at Balmoral, I've been told,
And, mind ye, seldom silver,
    But very often gold.

I hope God will protect her
    By night and by day,
At home and abroad
    When she's far away.

May He be as a hedge around her,
    As He's been all along,
And let her live and die in peace
    Is the end of my song.

SAVING A TRAIN.

'TWAS In the year of 1869, and on the 19th of November,
Which the people in Southern Germany will long remember,
The great rain-storm which for twenty hours did pour down,
That the rivers were overflowed and petty streams all around.

The rain fell in such torrents as had never been seen before,
That it seemed like a second deluge, the mighty torrents' roar,
At nine o'clock at night the storm did rage and moan,
When Carl Springel set out on his crutches all alone—

From the handsome little hut in which he dwelt,
With some food to his father, for whom he greatly felt,
Who was watching at the railway bridge,
Which was built upon a perpendicular rocky ridge.

The bridge was composed of iron and wooden blocks,
And crossed o'er the Devil's Gulch, an immense cleft of rocks,
Two hundred feet wide and one hundred and fifty feet deep,
And enough to make one's flesh to creep.

Far beneath the bridge a mountain-stream did boil and rumble,
And on that night did madly toss and tumble;
Oh! it must have been an awful sight,.
To see the great cataract falling from such a height.

It was the duty of Carl's father to watch the bridge on stormy nights,
And warn the on-coming trains of danger with the red lights;
So, on this stormy night, the boy Carl hobbled along
Slowly and fearlessly upon his crutches, because he wasn't strong.

He struggled on manfully with all his might
Through the fearful darkness of the night,
And half-blinded by the heavy rain,
But still resolved the bridge to gain.

But, when within one hundred yards of the bridge, it gave way with an awful crash,
And fell into the roaring flood below, and made a fearful splash,
Which rose high above the din of the storm,
The like brave Carl never heard since he was born.

Then father! father! cried Carl in his loudest tone,
Father! father! he shouted again in very pitiful moans;
But no answering voice did reply,
Which caused him to heave a deep-fetched sigh.

And now to brave Carl the truth was clear
That he had lost his father dear,
And he cried, My poor father's lost, and cannot be found;
He's gone down with the bridge, and has been drowned.

But he resolves to save the on-coming train,
So every nerve and muscle he does strain,
And he trudges along dauntlessly on his crutches,
And tenaciously to them he clutches.

And just in time he reaches his father's car
To save the on-coming train from afar,
So he seizes the red light, and swings it round,
And cries with all his might, The bridge is down! The bridge is down!

So forward his father's car he drives,
Determined to save the passengers' lives,
Struggling hard with might and main,
Hoping his struggle won't prove in vain.

So on comes the iron-horse snorting and rumbling,
And the mountain-torrent at the bridge kept roaring and tumbling;
While brave Carl keeps shouting, The bridge is down! The bridge is down!
He cried with a pitiful wail and sound.

But, thank heaven, the engine-driver sees the red light
That Carl keeps swinging round his head with all his might,
But bang! bang! goes the engine with a terrible crash,
And the car is dashed all to smash.

But the breaking of the car stops the train,
And poor Carl's struggle is not in vain;
But, poor soul, he was found stark dead,
Crushed and mangled from foot to head!

And the passengers were all loud in Carl's praise,
And from the cold wet ground they did him raise,
And tears for brave Carl fell silently around,
Because he had saved two hundred passengers from being drowned.

In a quiet village cemetery he now sleeps among the silent dead,
In the south of Germany, with a tombstone at his head,
Erected by the passengers he saved in the train,
And which to his memory will long remain.

THE MOON.

BEAUTIFUL Moon, with thy silvery light,
Thou seemest most charming to my sight;
As I gaze upon thee in the sky so high,
A tear of joy does moisten mine eye.

Beautiful Moon, with thy silvery light,
Thou cheerest the Esquimau in the night;
For thou lettest him see to harpoon the fish,
And with them he makes a dainty dish.

Beautiful Moon, with thy silvery light,
Thou cheerest the fox in the night,
And lettest him see to steal the grey goose away
Out of the farm-yard from a stack of hay.

Beautiful Moon, with thy silvery light,
Thou cheerest the farmer in the night,
And makest his heart beat high with delight
As he views his crops by the light in the night.

Beautiful Moon, with thy silvery light,
Thou cheerest the eagle in the night,
And lettest him see to devour his prey,
And carry it to his nest away.

Beautiful Moon, with thy silvery light,
Thou cheerest the mariner in the night
As he paces the deck alone,
Thinking of his dear friends at home.

Beautiful Moon, with thy silvery light,
Thou cheerest the weary traveller in the night;
For thou lightest up the wayside around
To him when he is homeward bound.

Beautiful Moon, with thy silvery light,
Thou cheerest the lovers in the night
As they walk through the shady groves alone,
Making love to each other before they go home.

Beautiful Moon, with thy silvery light,
Thou cheerest the poacher in the night;
For thou lettest him see to set his snares
To catch the rabbits and the hares.

THE BEAUTIFUL SUN.

Beautiful Sun! with thy golden rays,
To God, the wise Creator, be all praise;
For thou nourisheth all the creation,
Wherever there is found to be animation.

Without thy heat we could not live,
Then praise to God we ought to give ;
For thou makest the fruits and provisions to grow,
To nourish all creatures on earth below.

Thou makest the hearts of the old feel glad,
Likewise the young child and the lad,
And the face of Nature to look green and gay,
And the little children to sport and play.

Thou also giveth light unto the Moon,
Which certainly is a very great boon
To all God's creatures here below,
Throughout the world where'er they go.

How beautiful thou look'st on a summer morn,
When thou sheddest thy effulgence among the yellow corn,
Also upon lake, and river, and the mountain tops,
Whilst thou lea vest behind the most lovely dewdrops!

How beautiful thou seem'st in the firmament above,
As I gaze upon thee, my heart fills with love
To God, the great Creator, Who has placed thee there,
Who watches all His creatures with an eye of care!

Thou makest the birds to sing on the tree,
Also by meadow, mountain, and lea;
And the lark high poised up in air,
Carolling its little song with its heart free from care.

Thou makest the heart of the shepherd feel gay
As he watches the little lambkins at their innocent play;
While he tends them on the hillside all day,
Taking care that none of them shall go astray.

Thou cheerest the weary traveller while on his way
During the livelong summer day,
As he admires the beautiful scenery while passing along,
And singing to himself a stave of a song.

Thou cheerest the tourist while amongst the Highland hills,
As he views their beautiful sparkling rills
Glittering like diamonds by thy golden rays,
While the hills seem to offer up to God their praise.

While the bee from flower to flower does roam
To gather honey, and carry it home;
While it hums its little song in the beautiful sunshine,
And seemingly to thank the Creator divine—

For the honey it hath gathered during the day,
In the merry month of May,
When the flowers are in full bloom,
Also the sweet honeysuckle and the broom.

How beautiful thy appearance while setting in the west,
Whilst encircled with red and azure, 'tis then thou look'st best!
Then let us all thank God for thy golden light
In our prayers every morning and night!

GRACE DARLING;

OR,

THE WRECK OF THE "FORFARSHIRE."

As the night was beginning to close in one rough September day
In the year of 1838, a steamer passed through the Fairway
Between the Fame Islands and the coast, on her passage northwards;
But the wind was against her, and the steamer laboured hard.

There she laboured in the heavy sea against both wind and tide,
While a dense fog enveloped her on every side;
And the mighty billows made her timbers creak,
Until at last, unfortunately, she sprung a leak.

Then all hands rushed to the pumps, and wrought with might and main.
But the water, alas! alarmingly on them did gain;
And the thick sleet was driving across the raging sea,
While the wind it burst upon them in all its fury.

And the fearful gale and the murky aspect of the sky
Caused the passengers on board to lament and sigh
As the sleet drove thick, furious, and fast,
And as the waves surged mountains high, they stood aghast.

And the screaming of the sea-birds foretold a gathering storm,
And the passengers, poor souls, looked pale and forlorn,
And on every countenance was depicted woe
As the "Forfarshire" steamer was pitched to and fro.

And the engine-fires with the water were washed out;
Then, as the tide set strongly in, it wheeled the vessel about,
And the ill-fated vessel drifted helplessly along;
But the fog cleared up a little as the night wore on.

Then the terror-stricken crew saw the breakers ahead,
And all thought of being saved from them fled;
And the Fame lights were shining hazily through the gloom,
While in the fore-cabin a woman lay with two children in a swoon.

Before the morning broke, the "Forfarshire" struck upon a rock,
And was dashed to pieces by a tempestuous shock,
Which raised her for a moment, and dashed her down again,
Then the ill-starred vessel was swallowed up in the briny main.

Before the vessel broke up, some nine or ten of the crew intent
To save their lives, or perish in the attempt,
Lowered one of the boats while exhausted and forlorn,
And, poor souls, were soon lost sight of in the storm.

Around the windlass on the forecastle some dozen poor wretches clung,
And with despair and grief their weakly hearts were rung
As the merciless sea broke o'er them every moment;
But God in His mercy to them Grace Darling sent.

By the first streak of dawn she early up had been,
And happened to look out upon the stormy scene,
And she descried the wreck through the morning gloom;
But she resolved to rescue them from such a perilous doom.

Then she cried, Oh! father dear, come here and see the wreck,
See, here take the telescope, and you can inspect;
Oh! father, try and save them, and heaven will you bless;
But, my darling, no help can reach them in such a storm as this.

Oh! my kind father, you will surely try and save
These poor souls from a cold and watery grave;
Oh! I cannot sit to see them perish before mine eyes,
And, for the love of heaven, do not my pleading despise!

Then old Darling yielded, and launched the little boat,
And high on the big waves the boat did float;
Then Grace and her father took each an oar in hand,
And to see Grace Darling rowing the picture was grand.

And as the little boat to the sufferers drew near,
Poor souls, they tried to raise a cheer;
But as they gazed upon the heroic Grace,
The big tears trickled down each sufferer's face.

And nine persons were rescued almost dead with the cold
By modest and lovely Grace Darling, that heroine bold;
The survivors were taken to the light-house, and remained there two days,
And every one of them was loud in Grace Darling's praise.

Grace Darling was a comely lass, with long, fair floating hair,
With soft blue eyes, and shy, and modesty rare;
And her countenance was full of sense and genuine kindliness,
With a noble heart, and ready to help suffering creatures in distress.

But, alas! three years after her famous exploit,
Which, to the end of time, will never be forgot,
Consumption, that fell destroyer, carried her away
To heaven, I hope, to be an angel for ever and aye.

Before she died, scores of suitors in marriage sought her hand;
But no, she'd rather live in Longstone light-house on Fame island,
And there she lived and died with her father and mother,
And for her equal in true heroism we cannot find another.

TO MR JAMES SCRYMGEOUR, DUNDEE.

SUCCESS to James Scrymgeour,
    He's a very good man,
And to gainsay it,
    There's few people can ;

Because he makes the hearts
    Of the poor o'erjoyed
By trying to find work for them
    When they're unemployed.

And to their complaints
    He has always an attentive ear,
And ever ready to help the
    When unto him they draw near.

And no matter what your occupation is,
    Or what is your creed,
He will try to help you
    In the time of need;

Because he has the fear
    Of God within his heart,
And the man that fears God
    Always takes the poor's part.

And blessed is the man
    That is kind to the poor;
For his reward in heaven,
    'Tis said in the Scripture, is sure.

And I hope heaven will be
    Mr James Scrymgeour's reward;
For his struggles on behalf of the poor
    Are really vexatious and hard.

For he is to be seen daily
    Walking along our streets,
With a Christian-looking countenance,
    And a kind word to all he meets.

Besides, he is void of all pride,
    And wouldn't feel ashamed
To be seen with a beggar
    Or a tinker walking by his side.

Fellow-citizens of Dundee,
    Isn't it really very nice
To think of James Scrymgeour trying
    To rescue fallen creatures from the paths of vice?

And in the winter he tries to provide
    Hot dinners for the poor children of Dundee,
Who are starving with hunger no doubt,
    And in the most abject poverty.

He is a little deaf, no doubt,
    But not deaf to the cries of hungry men;
No! he always tries to do his best
    To procure bread for them.

And at the Sabbath-morning free-breakfasts
    He is often seen there,
Administering to the wants of the hungry,
    And joining in prayer.

He is a man of noble principles,
    As far as I can think,
And the noblest principle he has got
    Is, he abhors the demon drink.

And, in my opinion, he is right
    As far as I can see,
And I hereby proclaim that such a man
    Is an honour to Dundee:

Because he is always working
    For the poor people's good,
Kind soul, trying hard
    To procure for them clothing and food.

Success to him and his family,
    And may God them defend:
Why? fellow-citizens of Dundee,
    Because he is the poor man's friend.

THE BATTLE OF BANNOCKBURN.

Sir Robert the Bruce at Bannockburn
Beat the English in every wheel and turn,
And made them fly in great dismay
From off the field without delay.

The English were a hundred thousand strong,
And King Edward passed through the Lowlands all along,
Determined to conquer Scotland, it was his desire,
And then to restore it to his own empire.

King Edward brought numerous waggons in his train,
Expecting that most of the Scottish army would be slain,
Hoping to make the rest prisoners, and carry them away
In waggon-loads to London without delay.

The Scottish army did not amount to more than thirty thousand strong;
But Bruce had confidence he'd conquer his foes ere long;
So, to protect his little army, he thought it was right
To have deep-dug pits made in the night;

And caused them to be overlaid with turf and brushwood
Expecting the plan would prove effectual where his little army stood,
Waiting patiently for the break of day,
All willing to join in the deadly fray.

Bruce stationed himself at the head of the reserve,
Determined to conquer, but never to swerve,
And by his side were brave Kirkpatrick and true De Longueville,
Both trusty warriors, firm and bold, who would never him beguile.

By daybreak the whole of the English army came in view,
Consisting of archers and horsemen, bold and true;
The main body was led on by King Edward himself,
An avaricious man, and fond of pelf.

The Abbot of Inchaffray celebrated mass,
And all along the Scottish lines barefoot he did pass,
With the crucifix in his hand, a most beautiful sight to see,
Exhorting them to trust in God, and He would set them free.

Then the Scottish army knelt down on the field,
And King Edward he thought they were going to yield,
And he felt o'erjoyed, and cried to Earl Percy,
"See! See! the Scots are crying for mercy."

But Percy said, "Your Majesty need not make such a fuss,
They are crying for mercy from God, not from us;
For, depend upon it, they will fight to a man, and find their graves
Rather than yield to become your slaves."

Then King Edward ordered his horsemen to charge,
Thirty thousand in number, it was very large;
They thought to o'erwhelm them ere they could rise from their knees,
But they met a different destiny, which did them displease;
For the horsemen fell into the spik'd pits in the way,
And, with broken ranks and confusion, they all fled away.

But few of them escap'd death from the spik'd pits,
For the Scots with their swords hack'd them to bits;
De Valence was overthrown and carried off the field
Then King Edward he thought it was time to yield.

And he uttered a fearful cry
To his gay archers near by,
Ho! archers! draw your arrows to the head,
And make sure to kill them dead;
Forward, without dread, and make them fly,
Saint George for England, be our cry!

Then the arrows from their bows swiftly did go,
And fell amongst them as thick as the flakes of snow;
Then Bruce he drew his trusty blade,
And in heroic language said,
Forward! my heroes, bold and true!
And break the archers' ranks through and through!
And charge them boldly with your swords in hand,
And chase these vultures from off our land,
And make King Edward mourn
The day he came to Bannockburn.

See proud Edward on his milk-white steed,
One of England's finest breed,
Coming here in grand array,
With horsemen bold and archers gay,
Thinking he will us dismay,
And sweep everything before him in his way;
But I swear by yon blessed sun
I'll make him and his army run
From off the field of Bannockburn.

By St. Andrew and our God most high,
We'll conquer these epicures or die!
And make them fly like chaff before the wind
Until they can no refuge find;
And beat them off the field without delay,
Like lions bold and heroes gay.
Upon them!—charge!—follow me,
For Scotland's rights and liberty!

Then the Scots charged them with sword in hand,
And made them fly from off their land;
And King Edward was amazed at the sight,
And he got wounded in the fight;
And he cried, Oh, heaven! England's lost, and I'm undona,
Alas! alas! where shall I run?
Then he turned his horse, and rode on afar,
And never halted till he reached Dunbar.

Then Bruce he shouted, Victory!
We have gained our rights and liberty;
And thanks be to God above
That we have conquered King Edward this day,
A usurper that does not us love.

Then the Scots did shout and sing,
Long live Sir Robert Bruce our King!
That made King Edward mourn
The day he came to Bannockburn!

EDINBURGH.

BEAUTIFUL city of Edinburgh!
Where the tourist can drown his sorrow
By viewing your monuments and statues fine
During the lovely summer-time.
I'm sure it will his spirits cheer
As Sir Walter Scott's monument he draws near,
That stands in East Princes Street
Amongst flowery gardens, fine and neat.
And Edinburgh castle is magnificent to be seen
With its beautiful walks and trees so green,
Which seems like a fairy dell;
And near by its rocky basement is St. Margaret's well,
Where the tourist can drink at when he feels dry,
And view the castle from beneath so very high,
Which seems almost towering to the sky.
Then as for Nelson's monument that stands on the Calton hill,
As the tourist gazes thereon, with wonder his heart does fill
As he thinks on Admiral Nelson who did the Frenchmen kill.
Then, as for Salisbury crags, they are most beautiful to be seen,
Especially in the month of June, when the grass is green;
There numerous mole-hills can be seen,
And the busy little creatures howking away,
Searching for worms amongst the clay;
And as the tourist's eye does wander to and fro
From the south side of Salisbury crags below,
His bosom with admiration feels all aglow
As he views the beautiful scenery in the valley below;
And if, with an observant eye, the little loch beneath he scans,
He can see the wild ducks swimming about and beautiful white swans.
Then, as for Arthur's seat, I'm sure it is a treat
Most worthy to be seen, with its rugged rocks and pastures green,
And the sheep browsing on its sides
To and fro, with slow-paced strides,
And the little lambkins at play
During the livelong summer-day.
Beautiful city of Edinburgh! the truth to express,
Your beauties are matchless I must confess,
And which no one dare gainsay,
But that you are the grandest city in Scotland at the present day!

GLASGOW.

BEAUTIFUL city of Glasgow, with your streets so neat and clean,
Your stately mansions, and beautiful Green!
Likewise your beautiful bridges across the river Clyde,
And on your bonnie banks I would like to reside.

Chorus—
Then away to the West—to the beautiful West!
To the fair city of Glasgow that I like the best,
Where the river Clyde rolls on to the sea,
And the lark and the blackbird whistle with glee.

'Tis beautiful to see the ships passing to and fro,
Laden with goods for the high and the low;
So let the beautiful city of Glasgow flourish,
And may the inhabitants always find food their bodies to nourish.
Chorus

The statue of the Prince of Orange is very grand,
Looking terror to the foe, with a truncheon in his hand,
And well mounted on a noble steed, which stands in the Trongate,
And holding up its foreleg, I'm sure it looks first-rate.
Chorus.

Then there's the Duke of Wellington's statue in Royal Exchange Square—
It is a beautiful statue I without fear declare,
Besides inspiring and most magnificent to view,
Because he made the French fly at the battle of Waterloo.
Chorus.

And as for the statue of Sir Walter Scott that stands in George Square,
It is a handsome statue—few can with it compare,
And most elegant to be seen,
And close beside it stands the statue of Her Majesty the Queen.
Chorus.

Then there's the statue of Robert Burns in George Square,
And the treatment he received when living was very unfair;
Now, when he's dead, Scotland's sons for him do mourn,
But, alas! unto them he can never return.
Chorus.

Then as for Kelvin Grove, it is most lovely to be seen
With its beautiful flowers and trees so green,
And a magnificent water-fountain spouting up very high,
Where the people can quench their thirst when they feel dry
Chorus.

Beautiful city of Glasgow, I now conclude my muse,
And to write in praise of thee my pen does not refuse;
And, without fear of contradiction, I will venture to say
You are the second grandest city in Scotland at the present day!
      Chorus.

OBAN.

OH! beautiful Oban with your lovely bay,
Your surroundings are magnificent on a fine summer-day;
There the lover of the picturesque can behold,
As the sun goes down, the scenery glittering like gold.

And on a calm evening, behind the village let him climb the hill,
And as he watches the sun go down, with delight his heart will fill
As he beholds the sun casting a golden track across the sea,
Clothing the dark mountains of Mull with crimson brilliancy.

And on a sunny morning 'tis delightful to saunter up the Dunstaffnage road,
Where the green trees spread out their branches so broad;
And as you pass the Lovers' Loan your spirits feel gay
As you see the leaflet float lightly on the sunny pathway.

And when you reach the little gate on the right hand,
Then turn and feast your eyes on the scene most grand,
And there you will see the top of Balloch-an-Righ to your right,
Until at last you will exclaim, Oh! what a beautiful sight!

And your mind with wonder it must fill
As you follow the road a couple of miles further, till
You can see Bennefure Loch on the left hand,
And the Castle of Dunstaffnage most ancient and grand.

Then go and see the waters of Loch Etive leaping and thundering
And flashing o'er the reef, splashing and dundering,
Just as they did when Ossian and Fingal watched them from the shore,
And, no doubt, they have felt delighted by the rapids' thundering roar.

Then there's Ganevan with its sparkling bay,
And its crescent of silver sand glittering in the sun's bright array,
And Dunolly's quiet shores where sea crabs abide,
And its beautiful little pools left behind by the tide.

Then take a sail across to Kerrera some day,
And see Gylen Castle with its wild-strewn shore and bay,
With its gigantic walls and towers of rocks
Shivered into ghastly shapes by the big waves' thundering shocks.

Then wander up Glen Crootyen, past the old village churchyard,
And as you pass, for the dead have some regard;
For it is the road we've all to go,
Sooner or later, both the high and the low!

And as you return by the side of the merry little stream,
That comes trotting down the glen most charming to be seen,
Sometimes wimpling along between heather banks,
And slipping coyly away to hide itself in its merry pranks.

Then on some pleasant evening walk up the Glen Shellach road,
Where numberless sheep the green hillside often have trod,
And there's a little farmhouse nestling amongst the trees,
And its hazel woods climbing up the brae, shaking in the breeze.

And Loch Avoulyen lies like a silver sea with its forests green,
With its fields of rushes and headlands most enchanting to be seen,
And on the water, like a barge anchored by some dreamland shore,
There wild fowls sit, mirrored, by the score.

And this is beautiful Oban, where the tourist seldom stays above a night,
A place that fills the lover of the picturesque with delight;
And let all the people that to Oban go
View it in its native loveliness, and it will drive away all woe.

Oh! beautiful Oban, with your silvery bay,
'Tis amongst your Highland scenery I'd like to stray
During the livelong summer-day,
And feast my eyes on your beautiful scenery, enchanting and gay.

THE BATTLE OF FLODDEN FIELD.

'TWAS on the 9th of September, a very beautiful day,
That a numerous English army came in grand array,
And pitched their tents on Flodden field so green
In the year of our Lord fifteen hundred and thirteen.

And on the ridge of Braxton hill the Scottish army lay,
All beautifully arrayed, and eager for the fray,
And near by stood their noble king on that eventful day,
With a sad and heavy heart, but in it no dismay.

And around him were his nobles, both in church and state,
And they felt a little dispirited regarding the king's fate;
For the independence of bonnie Scotland was at stake,
And if they lost the battle, many a heart would break.

And as King James viewed the enemy he really wondered,
Because he saw by them he was greatly outnumbered,
And he knew that the struggle would be desperate to the last,
And for Scotland's weal or woe the die was cast.

The silence of the gathered armies was very still
Until some horsemen began to gallop about the brow of the hill,
Then from rank to rank the signal for attack quickly flew,
And each man in haste to his comrade closely drew.

Then the Scottish artillery opened with a fearful cannonade;
But the English army seemed to be not the least afraid,
And they quickly answered them by their cannon on the plain;
While innocent blood did flow, just like a flood of rain.

But the artillery practice very soon did cease,
Then foe met foe foot to foot, and the havoc did increase,
And, with a wild slogan cry, the Highlanders bounded down the hill,
And many of the English vanguard, with their claymores, they did kill.

Then, taken by surprise and the suddenness of the attack,
The vanguard of the English army instantly fell back,
But rallied again immediately—to be beaten back once more,
Whilst beneath the Highlanders' claymores they fell by the score.

But a large body of horsemen came to the rescue,
And the wing of the Scottish army they soon did subdue;
Then swords and spears clashed on every side around,
While the still air was filled with a death-wailing sound.

Then King James thought he'd strike an effective blow—
So he ordered his bodyguard to the plain below,
And all the nobles that were in his train,
To engage the foe hand to hand on that bloody plain.

And to them the din of battle was only a shout of glory;
But for their noble king they felt a little sorry,
Because they knew he was sacrificing a strong position,
Which was to his army a very great acquisition.

But King James was resolved to have his own will,
And he wouldn't allow the English to come up the hill,
Because he thought he wasn't matching himself equally against the foe;
So the nobles agreed to follow their leader for weal or woe.

'Twas then they plunged down into the thick of the fight,
And the king fought like a lion with all his might;
And in his cause he saw his nobles falling on every side around,
While he himself had received a very severe wound.

And the English archers were pouring in their shafts like hail,
And swords and spears were shivered against coats of mail,
And the king was manfully engaged contesting every inch of ground,
While the cries of the dying ascended up to heaven with a pitiful sound.

And still around the king the battle fiercely raged,
While his devoted followers were hotly engaged,
And the dead and the dying were piled high all around,
And alas! the brave king had received the second wound.

The Scottish army was composed of men from various northern isles,
Who had travelled, no doubt, hundreds of miles;
And with hunger and fatigue many were like to faint,
But the brave heroes uttered no complaint.

And heroically they fought that day on behalf of their king,
Whilst around him they formed a solid ring;
And the king was the hero of the fight,
Cutting, hacking, and slashing left and right.

But alas! they were not proof against the weapons of the foe,
Which filled their hearts with despair and woe;
And, not able to maintain their close form, they were beaten back,
And Lennox and Argyle, their leaders, were slain, alack!

And the field became so slippery with blood they could scarcely stand,
But in their stocking-feet they fought hand to hand,
And on both sides men fell like wheat before the mower,
While the cheers from both armies made a hideous roar.

Then King James he waved his sword on high,
And cried, "Scotchmen, forward! and make the Saxons fly;
And remember Scotland's independence is at stake,
So charge them boldly for Scotland's sake."

So grooms, lords, and knights fought all alike,
And hard blows for bonnie Scotland they did strike,
And swords and spears loudly did clatter,
And innocent blood did flow like water.

But alas! the king and his nobles fought in vain,
And by an English billman the king was slain;
Then a mighty cheer from the English told Scotland's power had fled,
And King James the Fourth of Scotland, alas! was dead!

GREENLAND'S ICY MOUNTAINS.

GREENLAND'S icy mountains are fascinating and grand,
And wondrously created by the Almighty's command;
And the works of the Almighty there's few can understand:
Who knows but it might be a part of Fairyland?

Because there are churches of ice, and houses glittering like glass,
And for scenic grandeur there's nothing can it surpass,
Besides there's monuments and spires, also ruins,
Which serve for a safe retreat from the wild bruins.

And there's icy crags and precipices, also beautiful waterfalls,
And as the stranger gazes thereon, his heart it appals
With a mixture of wonder, fear, and delight,
Till at last he exclaims, Oh! what a wonderful sight!

The icy mountains they're higher than a brig's topmast,
And the stranger in amazement stands aghast
As he beholds the water flowing off the melted ice
Adown the mountain sides, that he cries out, Oh! how nice!

Such sights as these are truly magnificent to be seen,
Only that the mountain tops are white instead of green,
And rents and caverns in them, the same as on a rugged mountain side,
And suitable places, in my opinion, for mermaids to reside.

Sometimes these icy mountains suddenly topple o'er
With a wild and rumbling hollow-startling roar;
And new peaks and cliffs rise up out of the sea,
While great cataracts of uplifted brine pour down furiously.

And those that can witness such an awful sight
Can only gaze thereon in solemn silence and delight,
And the most Godfearless man that hath this region trod
Would be forced to recognise the power and majesty of God.

Oh! how awful and grand it must be on a sunshiny day
To see one of these icy mountains in pieces give way!
While, crack after crack, it falls with a mighty crash
Flat upon the sea with a fearful splash.

And in the breaking up of these mountains they roar like thunder,
Which causes the stranger no doubt to wonder;
Also the Esquimaux of Greenland betimes will stand
And gaze on the wondrous work of the Almighty so grand.

When these icy mountains are falling, the report is like big guns,
And the glittering brilliancy of them causes mock-suns,
And around them there's connected a beautiful ring of light,

And as the stranger looks thereon, it fills his heart with delight.

Oh! think on the danger of seafaring men
If any of these mighty mountains were falling on them;
Alas! they would be killed ere the hand of man could them save,
And, poor creatures, very likely find a watery grave!

'Tis most beautiful to see and hear the whales whistling and blowing,
And the sailors in their small boats quickly after them rowing,
While the whales keep lashing the water all their might
With their mighty tails, left and right.

In winter there's no sunlight there night or day,
Which, no doubt, will cause the time to pass tediously away,
And cause the Esquimaux to long for the light of day,
So as they will get basking themselves in the sun's bright array.

In summer there is perpetual sunlight,
Which fill the Esquimaux' hearts with delight;
And is seen every day and night in the blue sky,
Which makes the scenery appear most beautiful to the eye.

During summer and winter there the land is covered with snow,
Which sometimes must fill the Esquimaux' hearts with woe
As they traverse fields of ice, ten or fifteen feet thick,
And with cold, no doubt, their hearts will be touched to the quick.

And let those that read or hear this feel thankful to God
That the icy fields of Greenland they have never trod;
Especially while seated around the fireside on a cold winter night,
Let them think of the cold and hardships Greenland sailors have to fight.

A TRIBUTE TO HENRY M. STANLEY,

THE GREAT AFRICAN EXPLORER.

WELCOME, thrice welcome, to the City of Dundee
The great African explorer, Henry M. Stanley,
Who went out to Africa its wild regions to explore,
And travelled o'er wild and lonely deserts, fatigued and footsore.

And what he and his little band suffered will never be forgot,
Especially one in particular, Major Edmund Barttelot,
Alas! the brave heroic officer by a savage was shot,
The commandant of the rear column—O hard has been his lot!

O think of the noble Stanley and his gallant little band,
While travelling through gloomy forests and devastated land,
And suffering from all kinds of hardships under a burning sun!
But the brave hero has been successful, and the victory's won!

While in Africa he saw many wonderful sights,
And was engaged, no doubt, in many savage fights,
But the wise Creator was with him all along,
And now he's home again to us, I hope quite strong.

And during his travels in Africa he made strange discoveries,
He discovered a dwarfish race of people called pigmies,
Who are said to be the original natives of Africa,
And when Stanley discovered them he was struck with awe.

One event in particular is most worthy to relate,
How God preserved him from a very cruel fate:
He and his officers were attacked, while sailing in their boat,
By the savages of Bumbireh, all eager to cut his throat.

They seized him by the hair, and tugged it without fear,
While one of his men received a poke in the ribs with a spear;
But Stanley, having presence of mind, instantly contrives
To cry to his men, Shove off the boat, and save your lives!

Then savages swarmed into three canoes very close by,
And every bow was drawn, while they savagely did cry;
But the heroic Stanley quickly shot two of them dead,
Then the savages were baffled, and immediately fled.

This incident is startling, but nevertheless true,
And in the midst of all dangers, the Lord brought him through,
Then, welcome him, thrice welcome him, right cheerfully,
Shouting, Long live the great African explorer, Henry M. Stanley!

Therefore throw open the gates of the City of Dundee,
And receive him with loud cheers, three times three,
And sound your trumpets and beat your drums,
And play up, See the Conquering Hero Comes!

JOTTINGS OF NEW YORK:

A DESCRIPTIVE POEM.

OH mighty City of New York! you are wonderful to behold,
Your buildings are magnificent, the truth be it told,
They were the only thing that seemed to arrest my eye,
Because many of them are thirteen storeys high.

And as for Central Park, it is lovely to be seen,
Especially in the summer season when its shrubberies and trees are green;
And the Burns' statue is there to be seen,
Surrounded by trees, on the beautiful sward so green;
Also, Shakespeare and Sir Walter Scott,
Which by Englishmen and Scotchmen will ne'er be forgot.

There the people on the Sabbath-day in thousands resort,
All loud in conversation and searching for sport,
Some of them viewing the menagerie of wild beasts there,
And also beautiful black swans, I do declare.

And there's beautiful boats to be seen there,
And the joyous shouts of the children do rend the air,
While the boats sail along with them o'er Lohengrin Lake,
And the fare is five cents for children and adults ten is all they take.

And there's also summer-house shades and merry-go-rounds,
And with the merry laughter of the children the Park resounds
During the livelong Sabbath-day,
Enjoying the merry-go-round play.

Then there's the elevated railroads, about five storeys high,
Which the inhabitants can see and hear night and day passing by,
Oh! such a mass of people daily do throng,
No less than five hundred thousand daily pass along,
And all along the City you can get for five cents,
And, believe me, among the passengers there are few discontent.

And the tops of the houses are all flat,
And in the warm weather the people gather to chat,
Besides on the house-tops they dry their clothes,
And also many people all night on the house-tops repose.

And numerous ships and steamboats are there to be seen,
Sailing along the East River Water so green;
'Tis certainly a most beautiful sight
To see them sailing o'er the smooth water day and night.

And Brooklyn Bridge is a very great height,
And fills the stranger's heart with wonder at first sight,
But with all its loftiness, I venture to say,
For beauty it cannot surpass the new Railway Bridge of the Silvery Tay.

And there's also ten thousand rumsellers there,
Oh! wonderful to think, I do declare!
To accommodate the people of that city therein,
And to encourage them to commit all sorts of sin.

And on the Sabbath-day, ye will see many a man
Going for beer with a tin can,
And seems proud to be seen carrying home the beer
To treat his neighbours and family dear.

Then at night numbers of the people dance and sing,
Making the walls of their houses to ring
With their songs and dancing on Sabbath night,
Which I witnessed with disgust, and fled from the sight.

And with regard to New York and the sights I did see,
One street in Dundee is more worth to me,
And, believe me, the morning I sailed from New York
For Bonnie Dundee, my heart it felt as light as a cork.

BEAUTIFUL MONIKIE.

BEAUTIFUL Monikie! with your trees and shrubberies green,
And your beautiful walks, most charming to be seen:
'Tis a beautiful place for pleasure-seekers to resort,
Because there they can have innocent sport,
By taking a leisure walk all round about,
And see the anglers fishing in the pond for trout.

Besides, there's lovely white swans swimming on the pond,
And Panmure Monument can be seen a little distance beyond;
And the scenery all round is enchanting I declare,
While sweet-scented fragrance fills the air.

Then away, pleasure-seekers of bonnie Dundee,
And have a day's outing around Monikie,
And inhale the pure air, on a fine summer day,
Which will help to drive dull care away;
As ye gaze on the beautiful scenery there,
Your spirits will feel o'erjoyed and free from care.

Then near to the pond there's a beautiful green sward,
Where excursionists can dance until fatigue does them retard:
And if they feel thirsty, the Monikie water's near by,
Where they can quench their thirst if very dry.

Then, after that, they can have a walk at their ease,
Amongst the green shrubbery and tall pine trees;
And in the centre of the pond they can see
Three beautiful little islets dressed in green livery.

Monikie is as bonnie a place as ye could wish to see,
And about eleven or twelve miles from bonnie Dundee;
It's the only place I know of to enjoy a holiday,
Because there's a hall of shelter there to keep the rain away.

Then there's a large park, a very suitable place,
For the old and the young, if they wish to try a race;
It's there they can enjoy themselves during the live-long summer day,
Near to the little purling burn, meandering on its way,
And emptying itself into the pond of Monikie,
Which supplies the people with water belonging Dundee.

A TRIBUTE TO MR MURPHY AND THE BLUE RIBBON ARMY.

ALL hail to Mr Murphy, he is a hero brave,
That has crossed the mighty Atlantic wave,
For what purpose let me pause and think—
I answer, to warn the people not to taste strong drink.

And, I'm sure, if they take his advice, they never will rue
The day they joined the Blue Ribbon Army in the year 1882;
And I hope to their colours they will always prove true,
And shout, Hurrah! for Mr Murphy and the Ribbon of Blue.

What is strong drink? Let me think—I answer 'tis a thing
From whence the majority of evils spring,
And causes many a fireside with boisterous talk to ring,
And leaves behind it a deadly sting.

Some people do say it is good when taken in moderation,
But, when taken to excess, it leads to tribulation,
Also to starvation and loss of reputation,
Likewise your eternal soul's damnation.

The drunkard, he says he can't give it up,
For I must confess temptation's in the cup;
But he wishes to God it was banished from the land,
While he holds the cup in his trembling hand.

And he exclaims in the agony of his soul—
Oh, God, I cannot myself control
From this most accurs'd cup!
Oh, help me, God, to give it up!

Strong drink to the body can do no good;
It denies the blood, likewise the food,
And causes the drunkard with pain to groan,
Because it extracts the marrow from the bone :

And hastens him on to a premature grave,
Because to the cup he is bound a slave;
For the temptation is hard to thole,
And by it he will lose his immortal soul.

The more's the pity, I must say,
That so many men and women are by it led astray,
And decoyed from the paths of virtue and led on to vice
By drinking too much alcohol and acting unwise.

Good people all, of every degree,
I pray, ye all be warned by me:
I advise ye all to pause and think,
And never more to taste strong drink.

Because the drunkard shall never inherit the kingdom of God
And whosoever God loves he chastens with his rod:
Therefore, be warned, and think in time,
And don't drink any more whisky, rum, or wine.

But go at once—make no delay,
And join the Blue Ribbon Army without dismay,
And rally round Mr Murphy, and make a bold stand,
And help to drive the Bane of Society from our land.

I wish Mr Murphy every success,
Hoping he will make rapid progress;
And to the Blue Ribbon Army may he always prove true,
And adhere to his colours—the beautiful blue.

LOCH KATRINE.

Beautiful Loch Katrine in all thy majesty so grand,
Oh! how charming and fascinating is thy silver strand!
Thou certainly art most lovely, and worthy to be seen,
Especially thy beautiful bay and shrubberies green.

> Then away to Loch Katrine in the summer time,
> And feast on its scenery most lovely and sublime;
> There's no other scene can surpass in fair Scotland,
> It's surrounded by mountains and trees most grand.

And as I gaze upon it, let me pause and think,
How many people in Glasgow of its water drink,
That's conveyed to them in pipes from its placid lake,
And are glad to get its water their thirst to slake.

> Then away to Loch Katrine in the summer time,
> And feast on its scenery most lovely and sublime;
> There's no other scene can surpass in fair Scotland,
> It's surrounded by mountains and trees most grand.

The mountains on either side of it are beautiful to be seen,
Likewise the steamers sailing on it with their clouds of steam:
And their shadows on its crystal waters as they pass along,
Is enough to make the tourist burst into song.

> Then away to Loch Katrine in the summer time,
> And feast on its scenery most lovely and sublime;
> There's no other scene can surpass in fair Scotland,
> It's surrounded by mountains and trees most grand.

'Tis beautiful to see its tiny wimpling rills,
And the placid Loch in the hollow of a circle of hills,
Glittering like silver in the sun's bright array,
Also many a promontory, little creek, and bay.

> Then away to Loch Katrine in the summer time,
> And feast on its scenery most lovely and sublime;
> There's no other scene can surpass in fair Scotland,
> It's surrounded by mountains and trees most grand.

Then to the east there's the finely wooded Ellen's Isle,
There the tourist can the tedious hours beguile,
As he gazes on its white gravelled beautiful bay,
It will help to drive dull care away.

> Then away to Loch Katrine in the summer time,
> And feast on its scenery most lovely and sublime;
> There's no other scene can surpass in fair Scotland,
> It's surrounded by mountains and trees most grand.

The mountains Ben-An and Ben-Venue are really very grand,
Likewise the famous and clear silver strand;
Where the bold Rob Roy spent many a happy day,
With his faithful wife, near by its silvery bay.

> Then away to Loch Katrine in the summer time,
> And feast on its scenery most lovely and sublime;
> There's no other scene can surpass in fair Scotland,
> It's surrounded by mountains and trees most grand.

FORGET-ME-NOT.

A GALLANT knight and his betroth'd bride,
Were walking one day by a river side,
They talk'd of love, and they talk'd of war,
And how very foolish lovers are.

At length the bride to the knight did say,
There have been many young ladies led astray
By believing in all their lovers said,
And you are false to me I am afraid.

No, Ellen, I was never false to thee,
I never gave thee cause to doubt me;
I have always lov'd thee and do still,
And no other woman your place shall fill.

Dear Edwin, it may be true, but I am in doubt,
But there's some beautiful flowers here about,
Growing on the other side of the river,
But how to get one, I cannot discover.

Dear Ellen, they seem beautiful indeed,
But of them, dear, take no heed;
Because they are on the other side,
Besides, the river is deep and wide.

Dear Edwin, as I doubt your love to be untrue,
I ask one favour now from you:
Go! fetch me a flower from across the river,
Which will prove you love me more than ever.

Dear Ellen! I will try and fetch you a flower
If it lies within my power * * *
To prove that I am true to you,
And what more can your Edwin do?

So he leap'd into the river wide,
And swam across to the other side,
To fetch a flower for his young bride,
Who watched him eagerly on the other side.

So he pluck'd a flower right merrily,
Which seemed to fill his heart with glee,
That it would please his lovely bride;
But, alas! he never got to the other side.

For when he tried to swim across,
All power of his body he did loss,
But before he sank in the river wide,
He flung the flowers to his lovely bride.

And he cried, Oh, Heaven! hard is my lot,
My dearest Ellen! Forget me not:
For I was ever true to you,
My dearest Ellen! I bid thee adieu!

Then she wrung her hands in wild despair,
Until her cries did rend the air;
And she cried, Edwin, dear, hard is our lot,
But I'll name this flower Forget-me-not.

And I'll remember thee while I live,
And to no other man my hand I'll give,
And I will place my affection on this little flower,
And it will solace me in a lonely hour.

THE ROYAL REVIEW:

AUGUST 25, 1881.

All hail to the Empress of India, Great Britain's Queen—
Long may she live in health, happy and serene—
That came from London, far away,
To review the Scottish Volunteers in grand array:
Most magnificent to be seen,
Near by Salisbury Crags and its pastures green,
Which will long be remembered by our gracious Queen—

And by the Volunteers, that came from far away,
Because it rain'd most of the day.
And with the rain their clothes were wet all through,
On the 25th day of August, at the Royal Review.
And to the Volunteers it was no lark,
Because they were ankle deep in mud in the Queen's Park,
Which proved to the Queen they were loyal and true,
To endure such hardships at the Royal Review.

Oh! it was a most beautiful scene
To see the Forfarshire Artillery marching past the Queen;
Her Majesty with their steady marching felt content,
Especially when their arms to her they did present.

And the Inverness Highland Volunteers seemed very gran',
And marched by steady to a man
Amongst the mud without dismay,
And the rain pouring down on them all the way.
And the bands they did play, God Save the Queen,
Near by Holyrood Palace and the Queen's Park so green.

Success to our noble Scottish Volunteers!
I hope they will be spared for many long years,
And to Her Majesty always prove loyal and true.
As they have done for the second time at the Royal Review,

To take them in general, they behaved very well,
The more that the rain fell on them pell-mell.
They marched by Her Majesty in very grand array,
Which will be remembered for many a long day,
Bidding defiance to wind and rain,
Which adds the more fame to their name.

And I hope none of them will have cause to rue
The day that they went to the Royal Review.
And I'm sure Her Majesty ought to feel proud,
And in their praise she cannot speak too loud,

Because the more that it did rain they did not mourn,
Which caused Her Majesty's heart with joy to burn,
Because she knew they were loyal and true
For enduring such hardships at the Royal Review.

THE NITHSDALE WIDOW AND HER SON.

'TWAS in the year of 1746, on a fine summer afternoon,
When trees and flowers were in full bloom,
That widow Riddelsat knitting stockings on a little rustic seat,
Which her only son had made for her, which was very neat.

The cottage she lived in was in the wilds of Nithsdale,
Where many a poor soul had cause to bewail
The loss of their shealings, that were burned to the ground,
By a party of fierce British dragoons that chanced to come round.

While widow Riddel sat in her garden she heard an unusual sound,
And near by was her son putting some seeds into the ground,
And as she happened to look down into the little strath below,
She espied a party of dragoons coming towards her very slow.

And hearing of the cruelties committed by them, she shook with fear.
And she cried to her son,' "Jamie, thae sodgers are coming here!"
While the poor old widow's heart with fear was panting,
And she cried, "Mercy on us, Jamie, what can they be wanting?"

Next minute the dragoons were in front of the cottage door,
When one of them dismounted, and loudly did roar,
"Is there any rebels, old woman, skulking hereabouts?"
"Oh, no, Sir, no! believe my word without any doubts."

"Well, so much the better, my good woman, for you and them;
But, old girl, let's have something to eat, me, and my men":
"Blithely, sir, blithely! ye're welcome to what I hae,"
When she bustled into the cottage without delay.

And she brought out oaten cakes, sweet milk, and cheese,
Which the soldiers devoured greedily at their ease,
And of which they made a hearty meal,
But, for such kind treatment, ungrateful they did feel.

Then one of the soldiers asked her how she got her living:
She replied, "God unto her was always giving;
And wi' the bit garden, alang wi' the bit coo,
And wi' what the laddie can earn we are sincerely thankfu'."

To this pitiful detail of her circumstances the villain made no reply,
But drew a pistol from his holster, and cried, "Your cow must die!"
Then riding up to the poor cow, discharged it through her head,
When the innocent animal instantly fell down dead.

Not satisfied with this the merciless ruffian leaped the little garden wall,
And with his horse trod down everything, the poor widow's all,
Then having finished this barbarous act of direst cruelty,
The monster rejoined his comrades shouting right merrily:

"There, you old devil, that's what you really deserve,
For you and your rascally rebels ought to starve";
Then the party rode off, laughing at the mischief that was done,
Leaving the poor widow to mourn and her only son.

When the widow found herself deprived of her all,
She wrung her hands in despair, and on God did call,
Then rushed into the cottage and flung herself on her bed,
And, with sorrow, in a few days she was dead.

And, during her illness, her poor boy never left her bedside,
There he remained, night and day, his mother's wants to provide,
And make her forget the misfortunes that had befallen them,
All through that villainous and hard-hearted party of men.

On the fourth day her son followed her remains to the grave.
And during the burial service he most manfully did behave,
And when the body was laid in the grave, from tears he could not refrain,
But instantly fled from that desolated place, and never returned again.

Thirteen years after this the famous battle of Minden was fought
By Prince Ferdinand against the French, who brought them to nought;
And there was a large body of British horse, under Lord George Sackville,
And strange! the widow's son was at the battle all the while.

And on the evening after the battle there were assembled in a tavern
A party of British dragoons, loudly boasting and swearing,
When one of them swore he had done more than any of them—
A much more meritorious action—which he defied them to condemn.

"What was that, Tarn, what was that, Tarn?" shouted his companions at once.
"Tell us, Tarn; tell us, Tarn, was that while in France?"
"No!" he cried, "it was starving an old witch, while in Nithsdale,
By shooting her cow and riding down her greens, that is the tale."

"And don't you repent it?" exclaimed a young soldier, present.
"Repent what?" cried the braggart; "No! I feel quite content."
"Then, villain!" cried the youth, unsheathing his sword,
"That woman was my mother, so not another word!

"So draw, and defend yourself, without more delay,
For I swear you shall not live another day!"
Then the villain sprang to his feet, and a combat ensued,
But in three passes he was entirely subdued.

Young Riddel afterwards rose to be a captain
In the British service, and gained a very good name
For being a daring soldier, wherever he went,
And as for killing the ruffian dragoon he never did repent.

JACK O' THE CUDGEL.

PART I.

'TWAS In the famous town of Windsor, on a fine summer morn,
Where the sign of Windsor Castle did a tavern adorn;
And there sat several soldiers drinking together,
Resolved to make merry in spite of wind or weather.

And old Simon the landlord was at the head of the table,
Cutting slices of beef as quick as he was able;
And one of the soldiers was of rather superior rank,
And on his dress trinkets of gold and silver together did clank.

He was a free companion, but surly and hard,
And a soldier of fortune, and was named Croquard;
And he had all the appearance of his martial calling,
But on this particular morning he was rudely bawling.

So the other soldiers laughed, for their spirits felt gay,
And they applauded his jokes, and let him have his own way,
Because he could command as desperate a gang of men as any in the world,
So many a joke and slur at the soldiers he hurled.

And the mirth increased as the day wore on,
And Croquard didn't seem the least woe-begone;
But, as he was trolling out a very merry song,
A wandering minstrel sat down beside him, and thought it no wrong.

By my troth, shouted Croquard, Come here, minstrel,
And give us a stave of love, or war, which is my will:
But the minstrel didn't appear to comply with this request;
And he tried to withdraw, as he thought it was best.

Ho! didst thou hear me, varlet? then Croquard did cry;
Oh! gentle sir, replied the minstrel, I cannot with your wish comply;
Believe me, I sing best to the ladies at the court,
And, in doing so, find it more profitable sport.

What, varlet! cried Croquard, Dost thou refuse me?
By heaven, proud cur, you shall see
And feel the weight of my hand before thou are much older:
Then he instantly sprang up, and seized the minstrel by the shoulder.

Then the youth began to tremble, and seemed terrified to death,
And appeared ready to faint for the want of breath;
While Croquard shook him roughly, just like an ugly whelp,
And he looked from one to another, imploring help.

At this moment a youth observed what was going on,
And he cried out to Croquard, Inhuman monster, begone!
Leave the minstrel, thou pig-headed giant, or I'll make you repent,
For thou must know my name is Jack, and I hail from Kent.

Then Croquard relaxed his hold of the minstrel boy,
Which caused the minstrel's heart to leap with joy;
As Jack placed himself before Croquard the giant,
And stood on his guard with a stout oak cudgel defiant.

Then the fist of the giant descended in a crack,
But Jack dealt Croquard a heavy blow upon the back
With his cudgel, so that the giant's hand fell powerless down by his side,
And he cursed and roared with pain, and did Jack deride.

Then the giant tried to draw his sword for to fight,
But Jack danced around him like a young sprite,
And struck him a blow with his cudgel upon the back of the head,
And from the effects of the blow he was nearly killed dead.

Then down sank the carcase of the giant to the ground,
While the soldiers about Jack did quickly gather round;
And Jack cried, Ha! lie thou there overgrown brute,
And defiantly he spurned Croquard's body with his foot.

There, lad, cried Vintner Simon, thou hast shown English spirit to-day,
By chastising yon overbearing giant in a very proper way;
So come, my lad, and drink a flagon of my very best sack,
For you handled your cudgel well, and no courage did lack.

Then no sooner had our hero finished his goblet of sack,
He cried, Go and fetch the minstrel back;
For the giant by this time had fled far away,
Therefore the minstrel's tender heart need not throb with dismay.

Then the minstrel was brought back without delay,
Which made Jack's heart feel light and gay;
And the minstrel thanked Jack for saving him on that eventful day,
So the soldiers drank to Jack's health, and then went away.

And when King Edward III. heard what Jack had done,
He sent for Jack o' the Cudgel, the noble Saxon,
And he made him his page, and Jack uttered not a word,
But he unwillingly gave up the cudgel for the honour of the sword.

PART II.

AFTER the battle of Calais, King Edward returns to fair England,
And he invited his nobles to a banquet most grand,
That the like hadn't been in England for many a day;
And many of the guests invited had come from far away.

The large hall of Windsor Castle was ablaze with light,
And there sat King Edward and his Queen, a most beautiful sight—
To see them seated upon two thrones of burnished gold;
And near the King sat Jack o' the Cudgel, like a warrior bold.

And when the banquet was prepared, King Edward arose,
And said, My honoured guests, I have called you together for a special purpose!
To celebrate our victories so gloriously achieved in France
By my noble and heroic troops, at the charge of the lance.

And now, since the war in France with us is o'er,
And Edward, our son, about to marry the lady he does adore,
The most amiable and lovely Countess of Kent;
Therefore, I hope they will live happy together and never repent.

Then King Edward took the Countess by the hand, and said,
Come, Edward, take your bride by the hand, and don't be afraid;
And do not think, my beloved son, that with you I feel wroth,
Therefore, take the Countess by the hand, and plight your troth.

Then the Prince arose and took the fair Countess by the hand,
As King Edward, his father, had given the royal command;
Then he led the Countess Joan to the foot of the throne,
Then King Edward and his Queen welcomed the Countess to their palatial home.

Then the Prince unto his father said, I must not forget, whatever betide,
That to Sir Jack o' the Cudgel I do owe my bride;
Because he rescued her from the hands of a fierce brigand,
Therefore 'twould be hard to find a braver knight in fair England.

Then a cheer arose, which made the lofty hall to ring,
As Jack advanced towards the throne, on the motion of the King;
Then Jack fell on one knee before King Edward,
Then said the Monarch, Arise, brave youth, and I will thee reward.

Sir Jack, I give thee land to the value of six hundred marks
In thine own native county of Kent, with beautiful parks,
Also beautiful meadows and lovely flowers and trees,
Where you can reside and enjoy yourself as you please.

And remember, when I need your service you will be at my command,
Then Jack o' the Cudgel bowed assent, and kissed King Edward's hand;
Then the Countess Joan took a string of rarest pearls from her hair,
And placed the pearls around Jack's neck, most costly and rare.

Then the tumult became uproarious when Jack received the presentation,
And he thanked the Lady Joan for the handsome donation;
Then all the ladies did loudly cheer, and on Jack smilingly did fan,
And Sir Walter Manny cried aloud, Sir Jack, you are a lucky man.

Then the mirth increased, and louder the applause,
And the Countess Joan asked, after a pause,
Tell me who has gained the love of the Knight o' the Cudgel;
Then Jack replied, My lady, you know her right well.

She is the lovely daughter of noble John of Aire,
Then, replied the Countess, she is a lovely creature, I must declare;
And I hope the choice that you have made won't make you grieve,
Then Jack kissed the Countess's hand, and took his leave.

And he wended his way to his beautiful estate in Kent,
And many a happy day there he spent;
And he married the lovely daughter of John of Aire,
And they lived happy together, and free from all care.

THE BATTLE OF CULLODEN:

A HISTOBICAL POEM.

'TWAS In the year of 1746, and in April the 14th day,
That Prince Charles Stuart and his army marched on without delay,
And on the 14th of April they encamped on Culloden Moor,
But the army felt hungry, and no food could they procure.

And the calls of hunger could not brook delay,
So they resolved to have food, come what may;
They, poor men, were hungry and in sore distress,
And many of them, as well as officers, slipped off to Inverness

The Prince gave orders to bring provisions to the field,
Because he knew without food his men would soon yield
To the pangs of hunger, besides make them feel discontent,
So some of them began to search the neighbourhood for refreshment.

And others, from exhaustion, lay down on the ground,
And soon in the arms of Morpheus they were sleeping sound;
While the Prince and some of his officers began to search for food,
And got some bread and whisky, which they thought very good.

The Highland army was drawn up in three lines in grand array,
All eager for the fray in April the 16th day,
Consisting of the Athole Brigade, who made a grand display
On the field of Culloden on that ever-memorable day.

Likewise the Camerons, Stewarts, and Macintoshes, Maclachlans and Macleans,
And John Roy Stewart's regiment, united into one, these are their names;
Besides the Macleods, Chisholms, Macdonalds of Clanranald and Glengarry,
Also the noble chieftain Keppoch, all eager the English to harry.

The second line of the Highland army formed in column on the right,
Consisting of the Gordons, under Lord Lewis Gordon, ready for the fight;
Besides the French Royal Scots, the Irish Piquets or Brigade,
Also Lord Kilmarnock's Foot Guards, and a grand show they made.

Lord John Drummond's regiment and Glenbucket's were flanked on the right
By Fitz-James's Dragoons and Lord Elcho's Horse Guards, a magnificent sight;
And on the left by the Perth squadron under Lord Strathallan,
A fine body of men, and resolved to fight to a man.

And there was Pitsligo, and the Prince's body guards under Lord Balmerino,
And the third line was commanded by General Stapleton, a noble hero;
Besides, Lord Ogilvy was in command of the third line or reserve,
Consisting of the Duke of Perth's regiment and Lord Ogilvy's—
    men of firm nerve.

The Prince took his station on a very small eminence,
Surrounded by a troop of Fitz-James's horse for his defence,
Where he had a complete view of the whole field of battle,
Where he could see the front line and hear the cannons rattle.

Both armies were about the distance of a mile from each other,
All ready to commence the fight, brother against brother,"
Each expecting that the other would advance
To break a sword in combat, or shiver a lance.

To encourage his men the Duke of Cumberland rode along the line,
Addressing himself hurriedly to every regiment, which was really sublime;
Telling his men to use their bayonets, and allow the Highlanders
    to mingle with them,
And look terror to the rebel foe, and have courage, my men.

Then Colonel Belford of the Duke's army opened fire from the front line,
After the Highlanders had been firing for a short time;
The Duke ordered Colonel Belford to continue the cannonade,
To induce the Highlanders to advance, because they seemed afraid.

And with a cannon-ball the Prince's horse was shot above the knee,
So that Charles had to change him for another immediately;
And one of his servants who led the horse was killed on the spot,
Which by Prince Charles Stuart was never forgot.

'Tis said in history, before the battle began
The Macdonalds claimed the right as their due of leading the van,
And because they wouldn't be allowed, with anger their hearts did burn,
Because Bruce conferred that honour upon the Macdonalds at
    the battle of Bannockburn.

And galled beyond endurance by the fire of the English that day,
Which caused the Highlanders to cry aloud to be led forward without delay,
"Until at last the brave Clan Macintosh rushed forward without dismay,
While with grape-shot from a side battery hundreds were swept away.

Then the Athole Highlanders and the Camerons rushed in sword in hand,
And broke through Barrel's and Monro's regiments, a sight most grand;
After breaking through these two regiments they gave up the contest,
Until at last they had to retreat after doing their best.

Then, stung to the quick, the brave Keppoch, who was abandoned by his clan,
Boldly advanced with his drawn sword in hand, the brave man.
But, alas! he was wounded by a musket-shot, which he manfully bore,
And in the fight he received another shot, and fell to rise no more.

Nothing could be more disastrous to the Prince that day,
Owing to the Macdonalds refusing to join in the deadly fray;
Because if they had all shown their wonted courage that day,
The proud Duke of Cumberland's army would have been forced to run away.

And, owing to the misconduct of the Macdonalds, the Highlanders had to yield,
And General O'Sullivan laid hold of Charles's horse, and led him off the field,
As the whole army was now in full retreat,
And with the deepest concern the Prince lamented his sore defeat.

Prince Charles Stuart, of fame and renown,
You might have worn Scotland's crown,
If the Macdonalds and Glengarry at Culloden had proved true;
But, being too ambitious for honour, that they didn't do,
Which, I am sorry to say, proved most disastrous to you,
Looking to the trials and struggles you passed through.

THE BATTLE OF SHERIFFMUIR:

A HISTORICAL POEM.

'TWAS in the year 1715, and on the 10th of November,
Which the people of Scotland have cause to remember;
On that day the Earl of Mar left Perth bound for Sheriffmuir,
At the same time leaving behind a garrison under Colonel Balfour.

Besides leaving a force of about three thousand men quartered
　　in different parts of Fife,
To protect the people's property, and quell party strife,
The army along with him amounted to three thousand foot
　　and twelve hundred cavalry,
All in the best of order, a most pleasant sight to see.

The two armies bivouacked near Sheriffmuir during the night,
And around their camp-fires they talked concerning the coming fight.
The Duke of Argyle's English army numbered eight thousand strong,
Besides four hundred horse, posted in the rear all along.

And the centre of the first line was composed often battalions of foot,
Consisting of about four thousand, under the command of Clanranald
　　and Glengarry to boot;
And at the head of these battalions Sir John Maclean and Brigadier Ogilvie,
And the two brothers of Sir Donald Macdonald of Sleat, all in high glee.

The Marquis of Huntly's squadron of horse was also there;
Likewise the Stirling squadron, carrying the Chevalier's standard, I do declare;
And the Perthshire squadron formed the left wing,
And with their boisterous shouts they made the welkin ring.

The centre of the second line consisted of eight battalions of infantry,
And three of the Earl of Seaforth's foot, famous for their bravery;
There were also two battalions of the Marquis of Huntly,
Besides the Earl of Panmure's battalion, all men of high degree

And those of the Marquis of Tullibardine, commanded by the
　　Viscount of Strathallan,
And of Logie Almond, and likewise Robertson of Strowan;
Besides two squadrons of horse under the Earl Marischal,
And the Angus squadron was on the left: these include them all.

During this formation, the Duke of Argyle was watching all the time,
But owing to the ground occupied by them he couldn't see their line,
Which was unfortunately obstructed by the brow of a hill,
At the thought thereof the Duke's heart with fear did fill.

The hill was occupied by a party of Earl Mar's troops looking towards Dunblane,
Which the Earl of Mar no doubt resolved to maintain;
Then the Duke returned to the army, and ordered the drums to beat,
But an hour elapsed before his army were ready Mar's to meet.

As soon as the Earl of Mar perceived Argyle's line was partially formed,
He gave orders that Argyle's army should be instantly stormed.
Then Mar placed himself at the head of the clans, and led forward his men,
As a noble hero would do, which no one can condemn.

Then he pulled off his hat, which he waved in his right hand,
And when he arrived within pistol-shot the Highlanders made a bold stand,
And they poured in a volley upon the English infantry,
And to the dismay of the Highlanders the English returned fire instantly.

And to the horror of the Highlanders Alan Muidartach was wounded mortally,
Then he was carried off the field, a most pitiful sight to see;
And as his men clustered around him they stood aghast,
And before he died he told them to hold their posts fast.

While lamenting the death of the Captain of Clanranald most pitifully,
Glengarry at this juncture sprang forward right manfully,
And throwing his bonnet into the air, he cried, heroically,
Revenge! revenge! revenge to-day! and mourning to-morrow ye shall see!

No sooner had he pronounced these words than the Highlanders rushed forward, sword in hand,
Upon the royal battalions with the utmost fury, which they could not withstand,
And with their broadswords among the enemy they spread death and dismay,
Until the three battalions on Argyle's left wing instantly gave way.

Then a complete rout ensued, and the Earl of Mar pursued them half-a-mile;
Then he ordered his men to halt and rest a while,
Until he should put them into order right speedily,
Then follow the enemy at the double-march and complete the victory.

Then the Highlanders chased them and poured in a volley'
Besides they hewed them down with their broadswords mercilessly;
But somehow both armies got mixed together, and a general rout ensued,
While the Highlanders eagerly the English army hotly pursued.

The success on either side is doubtful to this day,
And all that can be said is, both armies ran away;
And on whichsoever side success lay it was toward the Government,
And to allay all doubts about which party won, we must feel content.

THE EXECUTION OF JAMES GRAHAM, MARQUIS OF MONTROSE:

A HISTORICAL POEM.

'TWAS in the year of 1650, and on the twenty-first of May,
The city of Edinburgh was put into a state of dismay
By the noise of drums and trumpets, which on the air arose,
That the great sound attracted the notice of Montrose.

Who enquired at the Captain of the guard the cause of it,
Then the officer told him, as he thought most fit,
That the Parliament dreading an attempt might be made to rescue him,
The soldiers were called out to arms, and that had made the din.

Do I, said Montrose, continue such a terror still?
Now when these good men are about my blood to spill,
But let them look to themselves, for after I am dead,
Their wicked consciences will be in continual dread.

After partaking of a hearty breakfast, he commenced his toilet,
Which, in his greatest trouble, he seldom did forget.
And while in the act of combing his hair,
He was visited by the Clerk Register, who made him stare,

When he told him he shouldn't be so particular with his head,
For in a few hours he would be dead;
But Montrose replied, While my head is my own I'll dress it at my ease,
And to-morrow, when it becomes yours, treat it as you please.

He was waited upon by the Magistrates of the city,
But, alas! for him they had no pity.
He was habited in a superb cloak, ornamented with gold and silver lace:
And before the hour of execution an immense assemblage of people were round the place.

From the prison, bareheaded, in a cart, they conveyed him along the Watergate
To the place of execution on the High Street, where about thirty thousand people did wait,
Some crying and sighing, a most pitiful sight to see,
All waiting patiently to see the executioner hang Montrose, a man of high degree.

Around the place of execution, all of them were deeply affected,
But Montrose, the noble hero, seemed not the least dejected;
And when on the scaffold he had, says his biographer Wishart,
Such a grand air and majesty, which made the people start.

As the fatal hour was approaching when he had to bid the world adieu,
He told the executioner to make haste and get quickly through,
But the executioner smiled grimly, but spoke not a word,
Then he tied the Book of Montrose's Wars round his neck with a cord.

Then he told the executioner his foes would remember him hereafter,
And he was as well pleased as if his Majesty had made h m Knight of the Garter;
Then he asked to be allowed to cover his head,
But he was denied permission, yet he felt no dread.

He then asked leave to keep on his cloak,
But was also denied, which was a most grievous stroke;
Then he told the Magistrates, if they could invent any more tortures for him,
He would endure them all for the cause he suffered, and think it no sin.

On arriving at the top of the ladder with great firmness,
His heroic appearance greatly did the bystanders impress,
Then Montrose asked the executioner how long his body would be suspended,
Three hours was the answer, but Montrose was not the least offended.

Then he presented the executioner with three or four pieces of gold,
Whom he freely forgave, to his honour be it told,
And told him to throw him off as soon as he uplifted his hands,
While the executioner watched the fatal signal, and in amazement stands.

And on the noble patriot raising his hands, the executioner began to cry,
Then quickly he pulled the rope down from the gibbet on high,
And around Montrose's neck he fixed the rope very gently,
And in an instant the great Montrose was launched into eternity.

Then the spectators expressed their disapprobation by a general groan,
And they all dispersed quietly, and wended their way home,
And his bitterest enemies that saw his death that day,
Their hearts were filled with sorrow and dismay.

Thus died, at the age of thirty-eight, James Graham Marquis of Montrose,
Who was brought to a premature grave by his bitter foes;
A commander who had acquired great military glory
In a short space of time, which cannot be equalled in story.

BALDOVAN.

THE scenery of Baldovan
  Is most lovely to see,
Near by Dighty Water,
  Not far from Dundee.

'Tis health for any one
  To be walking there,
O'er the green swards of Baldovan,
  And in the forests fair.

There the blackbird and the mavis
  Together merrily do sing
In the forest of Baldovan,
  Making the woodlands to ring.

'Tis delightful to hear them
  On a fine summer day,
Carolling their cheerful notes
  So blythe and so gay.

Then there's the little loch near by,
  Whereon can be seen every day
Numerous wild ducks swimming
  And quacking in their innocent play.

LOCH LEVEN.

BEAUTIFUL Loch Leven, near by Kinross,
For a good day's fishing the angler is seldom at a loss,
For the loch it abounds with pike and trout,
Which can be had for the catching without any doubt;
And the scenery around it is most beautiful to be seen,
Especially the Castle, wherein was imprisoned Scotland's ill-starred Queen.

Then there's the lofty Lomond Hills on the eastern side,
And the loch is long, very deep, and wide;
Then on the southern side there's Benarty's rugged hills,
And from the tops can be seen the village of Kinross with its spinning mills.

The big house of Kinross is very handsome to be seen,
With its beautiful grounds around it, and lime trees so green;
And 'tis a magnificent sight to see, on a fine summer afternoon,
The bees extracting honey from the leaves when in full bloom.

There the tourist can enjoy himself and while away the hours,
Underneath the lime trees shady bowers,
And listen to the humming of the busy bees,
While they are busy gathering honey from the lime trees.

Then there's the old burying ground near by Kinross,
And the dead that lie there turned into dusty dross,
And the gravestones are all in a state of decay,
And the old wall around it is mouldering away.

MONTROSE.

BEAUTIFUL town of Montrose, I will now commence my lay,
And I will write in praise of thee without dismay,
And in spite of all your foes, .   .   .
I will venture to call thee Bonnie Montrose.
Your beautiful Chain Bridge is magnificent to be seen,
Spanning the river Esk, a beautiful tidal stream,
Which abounds with trout and salmon,
Which can be had for the catching without any gammon.

Then as for the Mid Links, it is most beautiful to be seen,
And I'm sure is a very nice bowling green,
Where young men can enjoy themselves and inhale the pure air,
Emanating from the sea and the beautiful flowers there,
And as for the High Street, it's most beautiful to see,
There's no street can surpass it in the town of Dundee,
Because it is so long and wide, .   .   .
That the people can pass on either side
Without jostling one another or going to any bother.

Beautiful town of Montrose, near by the seaside,
With your fine shops and streets so wide,
'Tis health for the people that in you reside,
Because they do inhale the pure fragrant air,
Emanating from the pure salt wave and shrubberies growing there;
And the inhabitants of Montrose ought to feel gay,
Because it is one of the bonniest towns in Scotland at the present day.

THE CASTLE OF MAINS.

ANCIENT Castle of the Mains,
With your romantic scenery
And surrounding plains,
Which seem most beautiful to the eye;
And the little rivulet running by,
Which the weary traveller can drink of when he feels dry,
And the heaven's breath smells sweetly there,
And scented perfumes fill the air,
Emanating from the green trees and beautiful wild flowers growing there.

There the people can enjoy themselves
And wile away the time,
By admiring the romantic scenery
In the beautiful sunshine;
And pull the little daisy,
As they carelessly recline
Upon the grassy green banks,
Which is most charming to see,
Near by the Castle of the Mains,
Not far from Dundee.

Then there's the old burying-ground,
Most solemn to see, . . .
And the silent dead reposing silently
Amid the shady trees,
In that beautiful fairy dell
Most lovely to see,
Which in the summer season
Fills the people's hearts with glee,
To hear the birds singing and the humming of the bee.

BROUGHTY FERRY.

Ancient Castle of Broughty Ferry
With walls as strong as Londonderry;
Near by the sea-shore,
Where oft is heard and has been heard the cannon's roar
In the present day and days of yore,
Loudly echoing from shore to shore.

From your impregnable ramparts high
Like the loud thunder in the sky,
Enough to frighten a foreign foe away
That would dare to come up the river Tay,
To lay siege to Bonnie Dundee,
I'm sure your cannon-balls would make them flee—

Home again to their own land
Because your cannon shot they could not withstand,
They would soon be glad to get away
From the beautiful shores of the silvery Tay.

Ancient Castle, near by Tayside,
The soldiers ought to feel happy that in you reside,
Because from the top they can have a view of Fife,
Which ought to drown their sorrow and give them fresh life,
And make their spirits feel light and gay
As they view the beautiful scenery of the silvery Tay.

The village of Broughty Ferry is most beautiful to see,
With its stately mansions and productive fishery,
Which is a great boon to the villagers and the people of Dundee,
And ought to make them thankful, and unto God to pray
For creating plenty of fish for them in the beautiful Tay.

And the city of Dundee seems beautiful to the eye
With her mill stalks and Old Steeple so high,
Which can be seen on a clear summer day
From the top of Broughty Castle near the mouth of Tay.

Then there's beautiful Reres Hill,
Where the people can ramble at their will
Amongst its beautiful shrubberies and trees so green
Which in the summer season is most charming to be seen,
And ought to drive dull care away,
Because the people can see every clear day
From the top the ships sailing on the silvery Tay.

ROBERT BURNS.

IMMORTAL Robert Burns of Ayr,
There's but few poets can with you compare;
Some of your poems and songs are very fine:
To "Mary in Heaven" is most sublime;
And then again in your "Cottar's Saturday Night,"
Your genius there does shine most bright,
As pure as the dewdrops of night.

Your "Tarn o' Shanter" is very fine,
Both funny, racy, and divine,
From John o' Groats to Dumfries
All critics consider it to be a masterpiece,
And, also, you have said the same,
Therefore they are not to blame.

And in my own opinion both you and they are right.
For your genius there does sparkle bright,
Which I most solemnly declare
To thee, Immortal Bard of Ayr!

Your "Banks and Braes of Bonnie Doon"
Is sweet and melodious in its tune,
And the poetry is moral and sublime,
And in my opinion nothing can be more fine.

Your "Scots wha hae wi' Wallace bled"
Is most beautiful to hear sung or read;
For your genius there does shine as bright,
Like unto the stars of night.   .   .

Immortal Bard of Ayr! I must conclude, my muse
To speak in praise of thee does not refuse,
For you were a mighty poet, few could with you compare,
And also an honour to Scotland, for your genius it is rare.

ADVENTURES OF KING ROBERT THE BRUCE.

King Robert the Bruce's deadly enemy, John of Lorn,
Joined the English with eight hundred Highlanders one fine morn,
All strong, hardy, and active fearless mountaineers,
But Bruce's men attacked them with swords and spears.

And while they were engaged, a new enemy burst upon them,
Like a torrent of raging water rushing down a rocky glen:
It was John of Lorn and his Highlanders that came upon them,
So the tide of battle was too much for them to stem.

And with savage yells they made the valley ring,
Then made a long circuit, and stole in behind the King,
Whirling their broadswords and Lochaber axes left and right;
And the enemy being thrice their number, they relinquished the fight.

Then to a certain house Bruce quickly hied,
And sitting by the door the housewife he spied;
And she asked him who he was, and he said, A wanderer,
Then she said, All wanderers are welcome here, kind sir.

Then the King said, Good dame, tell me the reason why,
How you respect all wanderers that chance to pass by,
And for whose sake you bear such favour to homeless men?
Then she said, King Robert the Bruce, if you want to ken,

The lawful King of this country, whom I hope to see;
Then Bruce said, My good woman, your King stands before thee;
And she said, Ah! sire, where are your men gone?
Then the King told her that he's come alone.

Then she said, Ah, my lawful King, this must not be,
For I have two stout sons, and they shall follow thee,
And fight to the death for your Majesty,
Aye, in faith, my good King, by land or sea.

Then she brought her sons before the King, and thus did say,
Now swear, my sons, to be true to your King without dismay;
Then they knelt and cried, Mother, we'll do as you desire.
We willingly will fight on behalf of our noble sire.

Who has been hunted like a felon by night and by day,
By foul plotters devising to take his life away;
But God will protect him in the midst of the strife,
And, mother dear, we'll fight for him during life.

Then the King said, Noble lads, it's you shall follow me,
And ye shall be near me by land or sea,
And for your loyalty towards me your mother I'll reward;
When all on a sudden the tramping of horses was heard.

Then the King heard voices he knew full well,
But what had fetched his friends there he couldn't tell;
'Twas Edward his brother and Lord Douglas, with one hundred and fifty men,
That had travelled far, to find their King, o'er mountain and glen.

And when they met they conversed on the events of the day,
Then the King unto them quickly did say,
If we knew where the enemy were, we would work them skaith;
Then Lord James said, I'll lead you where they are, by my faith.

Then they marched upon the enemy just as the morning broke,
To a farm-house where they were lodged, and, with one bold stroke,
They, the Scots, rushed in and killed two-thirds of them dead;
And such was the life, alas! King Robert the Bruce led!

A TALE OF THE SEA.

A PATHETIC tale of the sea I will unfold,
Enough to make one's blood run cold;
Concerning four fishermen cast adrift in a dory.
As I've been told, I'll relate the story.

'Twas on the 8th April, on the afternoon of that day,
That the little village of Louisburg was thrown into a wild state of dismay,
And the villagers flew to the beach in a state of wild uproar,
And in a dory they found four men were cast ashore.

Then the villagers, in surprise, assembled about the dory,
And they found that the bottom of the boat was gory;
Then their hearts were seized with sudden dread,
When they discovered that two of the men were dead.

And the two survivors were exhausted from exposure, hunger, and cold,
Which caused the spectators to shudder when them they did behold;
And with hunger the poor men couldn't stand on their feet,
They felt so weakly on their legs for want of meat.

They were carried to a boarding-house without delay,
But those that were looking on were stricken with dismay,
When the remains of James and Angus M'Donald were found in the boat,
Likewise three pieces of flesh in a pool of blood afloat.

Angus M'Donald's right arm was missing from the elbow,
And the throat was cut in a sickening manner, which filled the
    villagers hearts with woe,
Especially when they saw two pieces of flesh had been cut from each thigh,
'Twas then the kind-hearted villagers did murmur and sigh.

Angus M'Donald must have felt the pangs of hunger before he did try
To cut two pieces of flesh from James M'Donald's thigh;
But, Oh, heaven! the pangs of hunger are very hard to thole,
And anything that's eatable is precious unto an hungry soul.

Alas! it is most pitiful and horrible to think,
That with hunger Christians will each other's blood drink,
And eat each other's flesh to save themselves from starvation;
But the pangs of hunger makes them mad, and drives them to desperation.

An old American soldier, that had passed through the Civil War,
Declared the scene surpassed anything he's seen by far,
And at the sight, the crowd in horror turned away,
Which no doubt they will remember for many a day.

Colin Chisholm, one of the survivors, was looking very pale,
Stretched on a sofa, at the boarding-house, making his wail;

Poor fellow! his feet were greatly swollen, and with a melancholy air,
He gave the following account of the distressing affair:

We belonged to the American fishing schooner, named "Cicely,"
And our captain was a brave man, called M'Kenzie;
And the vessel had fourteen hands altogether,
And during the passage we had favourable weather.

'Twas on March the 17th we sailed from Gloucester, on the Wednesday,
And all our hearts felt buoyant and gay;
And we arrived on the Western banks on the succeeding Tuesday,
While the time unto us seemed to pass merrily away.

About eight o'clock in the morning, we left the vessel in a dory,
And I hope all kind Christians will take heed to my story:
Well, while we were at our work, the sky began to frown,
And with a dense fog we were suddenly shut down.

Then we hunted and shouted, and every nerve did strain,
Thinking to find our schooner, but, alas! it was all in vain:
Because the thick fog hid the vessel from our view,
And to keep ourselves warm we closely to each other drew.

We had not one drop of water, nor provisions of any kind,
Which, alas! soon began to tell on our mind:
Especially upon James M'Donald, who was very thinly clad,
And with the cold and hunger he felt almost mad.

And looking from the stern where he was lying,
He said, Good-bye, mates, Oh! I am dying!
Poor fellow, we kept his body, thinking the rest of us would be saved,
Then, with hunger, Angus M'Donald began to cry and madly raved.

And he cried, Oh, God! send us some kind of meat,
Because I'm resolved to have something to eat;
Oh! do not let us starve on the briny flood,
Or else I will drink of poor Jim's blood.

Then he suddenly seized his knife and cut off poor Jim's arm,
Not thinking in his madness he'd done any harm;
Then poor Jim's blood he did drink, and his flesh did eat,
Declaring that the blood tasted like cream, and was a treat.

Then he asked me to taste it, saying, It was good without doubt,
Then I tasted it, but in disgust I instantly spat it out;
Saying, If I was to die within an hour on the briny flood,
I would neither eat the flesh nor drink the blood.

Then in the afternoon again he turned to me,
Saying, I'm going to cut Jim's throat for more blood d'ye see;
Then I begged of him, for God's sake, not to cut the throat of poor Jim,
But he cried, Ha! ha! to save my own life I consider it no sin.

I tried to prevent him, but he struck me without dismay,
And cut poor Jim's throat in defiance of me, or all I could say,
Also a piece of flesh from each thigh, and began to eat away,
But poor fellow he sickened about noon, and died on the Sunday.

Now it is all over, and I will thank God all my life,
Who has preserved me and my mate, M'Eachern, in the midst
    of danger and strife;
And I hope that all landsmen of low and high degree,
Will think of the hardships of poor mariners while at sea.

DESCRIPTIVE JOTTINGS OF LONDON.

As I stood upon London Bridge and viewed the mighty throng
Of thousands of people in cabs and 'busses rapidly whirling along,
All furiously driving to and fro,
Up one street and down another as quick as they could go:

Then I was struck with the discordant sounds of human voices there,
Which seemed to me like wild geese cackling in the air:
And the river Thames is a most beautiful sight,
To see the steamers sailing upon it by day and by night.

And the Tower of London is most gloomy to behold,
And the crown of England lies there, begemmed with precious stones and gold;
King Henry the Sixth was murdered there by the Duke of Glo'ster,
And when he killed him with his sword he called him an imposter.

St. Paul's Cathedral is the finest building that ever I did see,
There's no building can surpass it in the city of Dundee,
Because it's magnificent to behold,
With its beautiful dome and spire glittering like gold.

And as for Nelson's Monument that stands in Trafalgar Square,
It is a most stately monument I most solemnly declare,
And towering defiantly very high,
Which arrests strangers' attention while passing by.

Then there's two beautiful water-fountains spouting up very high,
Where the weary traveller can drink when he feels dry;
And at the foot of the monument there's three bronze lions in grand array,
Enough to make the stranger's heart throb with dismay.

Then there's Mr Spurgeon, a great preacher, which no one dare gainsay,
I went to hear him preach on the Sabbath-day,
And he made my heart feel light and gay,
When I heard him preach and pray.

And the Tabernacle was crowded from ceiling to floor,
And many were standing outside the door;
He is an eloquent preacher I honestly declare,
And I was struck with admiration as on him I did stare.

Then there's Petticoat Lane I venture to say,
It's a wonderful place on the Sabbath-day;
There wearing-apparel can be bought to suit the young or old,
For the ready cash, silver, coppers, or gold.

Oh! mighty city of London! you are wonderful to see,
And thy beauties no doubt fill the tourist's heart with glee;
But during my short stay, and while wandering there,
Mr Spurgeon was the only man I heard speaking proper English I do declare.

ANNIE MARSHALL THE FOUNDLING.

ANNIE MARSHALL was a foundling, and lived in Downderry,
And was trained up by a coast-guardsman, kind-hearted and merry,
And he loved Annie Marshall as dear as his life,
And he resolved to make her his own loving wife.

The night was tempestuous, most terrific, and pitch dark,
When Matthew Pengelly rescued Annie Marshall from an ill-fated barque,
But her parents were engulfed in the briny deep,
Which caused poor Annie at times to sigh and weep.

One day Matthew asked Annie if she would be his wife,
And Annie replied, I never thought of it in all my life;
Yes, my wife, Annie, replied Matthew, hold hard a bit,
Remember, Annie, I've watched you grow up, and consider you most fit.

Poor Annie did not speak, she remained quite mute,
And with agitation she trembled from head to foot,
The poor girl was in a dilemma, she knew not what to say,
And owing to Matthew training her, she couldn't say him nay.

Oh! Matthew, I'm afraid I would not make you a good wife,
And in that respect there would be too much strife,
And the thought thereof, believe me, makes me feel ill,
Because I'm unfit to be thy wife, Matthew, faltered the poor girl.

Time will prove that, dear Annie, but why are you so calm?
Then Annie put her hand shyly into Matthew's brown palm.
Just then the flashing lightning played upon Annie's face,
And the loud thunder drowned Matthew's words as Annie left the place.

But Matthew looked after her as she went home straightway,
And his old heart felt light and gay,
As he looked forward for his coming marriage day,
Because he knew that Annie Marshall couldn't say him nay.

Then the sky grew dark, and the sea lashed itself into foam,
But he heeded it not as he sat there alone,
Till the sound of a gun came booming o'er the sea,
Then Matthew had to attend to his duty immediately.

A ship, he muttered, Lord, help them! and coming right in. by the sound,
And in a few minutes she will run aground.
And the vessel was dashed against the rocks with her helpless crew,
Then in hot haste for assistance Matthew instantly flew.

Then Matthew returned with a few men all willing to lend their aid,
But amongst them all Matthew seemed the least afraid;
Then an old man cried, Save my boy, for his mother's sake,
Oh! Matthew, try and save him, or my heart will break!

I will, Heaven helping me, Matthew said solemnly,
Come, bear a hand, mates, and lower me over the cliff quietly;
Then Matthew was lowered with ropes into what seemed a watery grave,
At the risk of his own life, old Jonathan Bately's son to save.

So Matthew Pengelly saved Jonathan Bately's son,
And the old man thanked God and Matthew for what he had done,
And the mother's heart was full of gratitude and joy,
For the restoration of her darling boy.

So Matthew resolved to marry Annie Marshall,
But first he'd go to sea whatever did befall,
To earn a few pounds to make the marriage more grand,
So he joined a whaling vessel and went to Greenland.

And while Matthew was away at Greenland,
David Bately wanted to marry Annie Marshall right offhand,
But Annie refused to marry David Bately,
So in anger David Bately went another voyage to sea.

A few nights after David Bately had gone to sea,
Annie's thoughts reverted to Matthew Pengelly,
And as she sat in the Downderry station watching the boiling waves below,
The wind blew a terrific gale, which filled her heart with woe.

And as she sat there the big waves did loudly roar,
When a man cried, Help! help! there's a corpse washed ashore;
Then Annie rushed madly to the little beach,
And when she saw the corpse she gave a loud screech.

So there is but little more to tell of this sad history,
Only that Annie Marshall mourned long for Matthew Pengelly,
Who had floated home to be buried amongst his own kin,
But, alas! the rest of the crew were buried in the sea, save him.

BILL BOWLS THE SAILOR.

'TWAS about the beginning of the present century,
Bill Bowls was pressed, and sent to sea;
And conveyed on board the Waterwitch without delay,
Scarce getting time to bid farewell to the villagers of Fairway

And once on board the "Waterwitch," he resolved to do his duty,
And God willing, he'd marry Nelly Blyth, the village beauty;
And he'd fight for Old England, like a jolly British tar,
And he'd think of Nelly Blyth during the war.

The poor fellow little imagined what he had to go through,
But in all his trials at sea, he never did rue;
No; the brave tar became reconciled to his fate,
And he felt proud of his commander, Captain Ward the great.

And on board the "Waterwitch "was Tom Riggles, his old comrade,
And with such a one as Tom Riggles he seldom felt afraid,
Because the stories they told on board made the time flyaway,
And made the hearts of their messmates feel light and gay.

'Twas on a sunny morning, and clear to the view,
Captain Ward the close attention of his men he drew:
Look! he cried, there's two Frenchmen of war on our right,
Therefore, prepare my men immediately to commence the fight.

Then the "Waterwitch" was steered to the ship most near,
While every man resolved to sell his life most dear;
But the French commander, disinclined to commence the fight,
Ordered his men to put on a press of canvas and take to flight.

But Captain Ward quickly gave the order to fire,
Then Bill Bowls cried, Now we'll get fighting to our heart's desire!
And for an hour and more a running fight was maintained,
Until the two ships of the enemy near upon the "Waterwitch" gained.

Captain Ward walked the deck with a firm tread,
When a shot from the enemy pierced the ship's side above his head;
And with a splinter Bill Bowls was wounded on the left arm,
And he cried, Death to the frog-eaters! they have done me little harm.

Then Captain Ward cried, Fear not, we will win the day,
Now, courage my men, pour in broadsides without delay;
Then they sailed round the "St. Denis" and the "Gloire,"
And in at their cabin windows they poured a deadly fire.

The effect on the two ships was fearful to behold,
But still the Frenchmen stuck to their guns with courage, be it told;
And the crash and din of artillery was deafening to the ear,
And the cries of the wounded men on deck were pitiful to hear.

Then Captain Ward to his men did say,
We must board these French ships without dismay;
Then he seized his cutlass, as he fearlessly spoke,
And jumped on board the "St. Denis" in the midst of the smoke.

Then Bill Bowls and Tom Riggles quickly followed him,
Then hand to hand the battle in earnest did begin;
And the men sprang upon their foes and beat them back,
And they hauled down their colours, and hoisted the Union Jack.

But the men on board the "St. Denis" fought desperately hard,
But, alas! as the "St. Denis" was captured, a ball struck Captain Ward
Right on the forehead, and he fell dead with a groan
And for the death of Captain Ward the sailors did cry and moan.

Then the first lieutenant, who was standing near by,
Loudly to the men did cry:
Come men, and carry your noble commander to his cabin below,
But there is one consolation, we have beaten the foe.

And thus fell Captain Ward in the prime of his life,
And I hope he is now in the better land, free from strife:
But, alas! 'tis sad to think he was buried in the mighty deep,
Where too many of our brave seamen do silently sleep.

The "St. Denis" and the "Gloire" were towed to Gibraltar, the nearest port,
But by the capturing of them, they felt but little sport,
Because, for the loss of Captain Ward, the men felt woebegone,
Because in bravery, they said, he was next to Admiral Nelson.

YOUNG MUNRO THE SAILOR.

'TWAS on a sunny morning in the month of May,
I met a pretty damsel on the banks o' the Tay;
I said, My charming fair one, come tell to me I pray,
Why you do walk alone on the banks o' the Tay.

She said, Kind sir, pity me, for I am in great woe
About my young sailor lad, whose name is James Munro;
It's he has been long at sea, seven years from this day,
And I come here sometimes to weep for him that's far, far away

Lovely creature, cease your weeping and consent to marry me,
And my houses and all my land I will give to thee,
And we shall get married without any delay,
And live happy and contented on the banks o' the Tay.

Believe me, my sweet lady, I pity the sailor's wife,
For I think she must lead a very unhappy life;
Especially on a stormy night, I'm sure she cannot sleep,
Thinking about her husband whilst on the briny deep.

Oh, sir! it is true, what you to me have said,
But I must be content with the choice I've made;
For Munro he's young and handsome, I will ne'er deny,
And if I don't get him for a husband, believe me, I will die.

Because, when last we parted, we swore to be true,
And I will keep my troth, which lovers ought to do;
And I will pray for his safe return by night and by day,
That God may send him safe home to the banks o' the Tay.

Forgive me, noble heart, for asking to marry you,
I was only trying your love, if it was really true;
But I've found your love is pure towards your sailor lad,
And the thought thereof, believe me, makes my heart feel glad.

As homeward we retraced our steps her heart seemed glad,
In hopes of seeing again her brave sailor lad,
Who had promised to marry her when he would return,
So I bade her keep up her spirits and no longer mourn.

Dear creature, the lass that's true to her sweetheart deserves great praise,
And I hope young Munro and you will spend many happy days,
For unto him I know you will ever prove true,
And perchance when he comes home he will marry you.

What you have said, kind sir, I hope will come true,
And if it does, I'll make it known to you;
And you must come to the marriage, which you musn't gainsay,
And dance and rejoice with us on the marriage-day.

When we arrived in Dundee she bade me good-bye,
Then I told her where I lived, while she said with a sigh,
Kind sir, I will long remember that morning in May,
When I met you by chance on the banks o' the Tay.

When three months were past her sailor lad came home,
And she called to see me herself alone,
And she invited me to her marriage without delay,
Which was celebrated with great pomp the next day.

So I went to the marriage with my heart full of joy,
And I wished her prosperity with her sailor boy;
And I danced and sang till daylight, and then came away,
Leaving them happy and contented on the banks o' the Tay.

So all ye pretty fair maids, of high or low degree,
Be faithful to your sweethearts when they have gone to sea,
And never be in doubts of them when they are far away,
Because they might return and marry you some unexpected day.

THE DEATH OF THE OLD MENDICANT.

THERE was a rich old gentleman
Lived on a lonely moor in Switzerland,
And he was very hard to the wandering poor,
'Tis said he never lodged nor served them at his door.

'Twas on a stormy night, and Boreas blew a bitter blast,
And the snowflakes they fell thick and fast,
When a poor old mendicant, tired and footsore,
Who had travelled that day fifteen miles and more,
Knocked loudly at the rich man's door.

The rich man was in his parlour counting his gold,
And he ran to the door to see who was so bold,
And there he saw the mendicant shivering with the cold

Then the mendicant unto him said,
My dear sir, be not afraid,
Pray give me lodgings for the night,
And heaven will your love requite;
Have pity on me, for I am tired and footsore,
I have travelled fifteen miles to-day and more.

Begone! you vagabond, from my door!
I never give lodgings to the poor;
So be off, take to your heels and run,
Or else I'll shoot you with my gun!
Now do not think I'm making fun;
Do you hear, old beggar, what I say?
Now be quick! and go away.

Have mercy, sir, I cannot go,
For I shall perish in the snow;
Oh! for heaven's sake, be not so hard,
And God will your love reward.

My limbs are tired, I cannot go away,
Oh! be so kind as let me stay.
'Twas vain! the rich man said, I shan't,
And shut his door on the mendicant,
And said, That is the way I'll serve the poor
While I live on this lonely moor.

Then the old mendicant did go away,
And, murmuring to himself, did say,
Oh, woe's me that ever I was born!
Oh, God, protect me from the storm!
My feeble limbs refuse to go,
And my poor heart does break with woe.

Then he lay down and died among the snow.
He was found by the rich man's shepherd next day,
While he was searching for sheep that had gone astray;
And he was struck with fear and woe
To see the body lying dead among the snow.

So the shepherd ran home and told his master
About the very sad disaster;
That he had found a dead body in the snow,
But whose it was he did not know.

Then the rich man ordered the body to be brought to his house,
And to be instantly dressed by his loving spouse,
For his conscience smote him with fear and woe,
When he heard of the old mendicant being found dead in the snow.

So the poor old mendicant was buried without delay
In a very respectable way;
And from that very day the rich man was kind to the poor
And never turned any one away from his door.

AN ADVENTURE IN THE LIFE OF KING JAMES V. OF SCOTLAND.

ON one occasion King James the Fifth of Scotland, when alone, in disguise,
Near by the Bridge of Cramond met with rather a disagreeable surprise.
He was attacked by five gipsy men without uttering a word,
But he manfully defended himself with his sword.

There chanced to be a poor man threshing corn in a barn near by,
Who came out on hearing the noise so high;
And seeing one man defending himself so gallantly,
That he attacked the gipsies with his flail, and made them flee.

Then he took the King into the barn,
Saying, "I hope, sir, you've met with no great harm;
And for five men to attack you, it's a disgrace;
But stay, I'll fetch a towel and water to wash your face."

And when the King washed the blood off his face and hands,
"Now, sir, I wish to know who you are," the King demands.
"My name, sir, is John Howieson, a bondsman on the farm of Braehead."
"Oh, well," replied the King, "your company I need not dread."

"And perhaps you'll accompany me a little way towards Edinburgh,
Because at present I'm not free from sorrow.
And if you have any particular wish to have gratified,
Let me know it, and it shall not be denied."

Then honest John said, thinking it no harm,
"Sir, I would like to be the owner of Braehead farm;
But by letting me know who you are it would give my mind relief."
Then King James he answered that he was the Gudeman of Ballingeich.

"And if you'll meet me at the palace on next Sunday,
Believe me, for your manful assistance, I'll you repay.
Nay, honest John, don't think of you I'm making sport,
I pledge my word at least you shall see the royal court."

So on the next Sunday John put on his best clothes,
And appeared at the palace gate as you may suppose.
And he inquired for the Gudeman of Ballingeich;
And when he gained admittance his heart was freed from grief.

For John soon found his friend the Gudeman,
And the King took John by the han',
Then conducted John from one apartment to another,
Just as kindly as if he'd been his own brother.

Then the King asked John if he'd like to see His Majesty.
"Oh, yes," replied John, "His Majesty I would really like to see."
And John looked earnestly into the King's face,
And said, "How am I to know His Grace?"

"Oh, John, you needn't be the least annoyed about that,
For all heads will be uncovered: the King will wear his hat."
Then he conducted John into a large hall',
Which was filled by the nobility, crown officers, and all.

Then said John to the King, when he looked round the room,
"Sir, I hope I will see the King very soon,"
Because to see the King, John rather dreaded,
At last he said to the King, "'Tis you! the rest are bareheaded."

Then the King said, "John, I give you Braehead farm as it stands,
On condition you provide a towel and basin of water to wash my hands,
If ever I chance to come your way."
Then John said, "Thanks to your Majesty, I'll willingly obey."

THE CLEPINGTON CATASTROPHE.

'TWAS on a Monday morning, and in the year of 1884,
That a fire broke out in Bailie Bradford's store,
Which contained bales of jute and large quantities of waste,
Which the brave firemen ran to extinguish in great haste.

They left their wives that morning without any dread,
Never thinking, at the burning pile, they would be killed dead
By the falling of the rickety and insecure walls;
When I think of it, kind Christians, my heart it appals!

Because it has caused widows and their families to shed briny tears,
For there hasn't been such a destructive fire for many years;
Whereby four brave firemen have perished in the fire,
And for better fathers or husbands no family could desire.

'Twas about five o'clock in the morning the fire did break out,
While one of the workmen was inspecting the premises round about—
Luckily before any one had begun their work for the day—
So he instantly gave the alarm without delay.

At that time only a few persons were gathered on the spot.
But in a few minutes some hundreds were got,
Who came flying in all directions, and in great dismay;
So they help'd to put out the fire without delay.

But the spreading flames, within the second flats, soon began to appear,
Which filled the spectators' hearts with sympathy and fear,
Lest any one should lose their life in the merciless fire,
When they saw it bursting out and ascending higher and higher.

Captain Ramsay, of the Dundee Fire Brigade, was the first to arrive,
And under his directions the men seemed all alive,
For they did their work heroically, with all their might and main,
In the midst of blinding smoke and the burning flame.

As soon as the catastrophe came to be known,
The words, Fire! Fire! from every mouth were blown;
And a cry of despair rang out on the morning air,
When they saw the burning pile with its red fiery glare.

While a dense cloud of smoke seemed to darken the sky,
And the red glaring flame ascended up on high,
Which made the scene appear weird-like around;
While from the spectators was heard a murmuring sound.

But the brave firemen did their duty manfully to the last,
And plied the water on the burning pile, copiously and fast;
But in a moment, without warning, the front wall gave way,
Which filled the people's hearts with horror and dismay:

Because four brave firemen were killed instantaneously on the spot,
Which by the spectators will never be forgot;
While the Fire Fiend laughingly did hiss and roar,
As he viewed their mangled bodies, with the *debris* covered o'er.

But in the midst of dust and fire they did their duty well,
Aye! in the midst of a shower of bricks falling on them pell-mell,
Until they were compelled to let the water-hose go;
While the blood from their bruised heads and arms did flow.

But brave James Fyffe held on to the hose until the last,
And when found in the *debris*, the people stood aghast.
When they saw him lying dead, with the hose in his hand,
Their tears for him they couldn't check nor yet command.

Oh, heaven! I must confess it was no joke
To see them struggling in the midst of suffocating smoke,
Each man struggling hard, no doubt, to save his life,
When he thought of his dear children and his wife.

But still the merciless flame shot up higher and higher;
Oh, God! it is terrible and cruel to perish by fire;
Alas! it was saddening and fearful to behold,
When I think of it, kind Christians, it makes my blood run cold.

What makes the death of Fyffe the more distressing,
He was going to be the groomsman at his sister's bridal dressing,
Who was going to be married the next day;
But, alas! the brave hero's life was taken away.

But accidents will happen by land and by sea,
Therefore, to save ourselves from accidents, we needn't try to flee,
For whatsoever God has ordained will come to pass;
For instance, ye may be killed by a stone or a piece of glass.

I hope the Lord will provide for the widows in their distress,
For they are to be pitied, I really must confess;
And I hope the public of Dundee will lend them a helping hand;
To help the widows and the fatherless is God's command.

THE REBEL SURPRISE NEAR TAMAI.

'TWAS on the 22nd of March, in the year 1885,
That the Arabs rushed like a mountain torrent in full drive,
And quickly attacked General M'Neill's transport-zereba,
But in a short time they were forced to withdraw.

And in the suddenness of surprise the men were carried away,
Also camels, mules, and horses were thrown into wild disarray,
By thousands of the Arabs that in ambush lay,
But our brave British heroes held the enemy at bay.

There was a multitude of camels heaped upon one another,
Kicking and screaming, while many of them did smother,
Owing to the heavy pressure of the entangled mass,
That were tramping o'er one another as they lay on the grass.

The scene was indescribable, and sickening to behold,
To see the mass of innocent brutes lying stiff and cold,
And the moaning cries of them were pitiful to hear,
Likewise the cries of the dying men that lay wounded in the rear.

Then General M'Neill ordered his men to form in solid square,
Whilst deafening shouts and shrieks of animals did rend the air,
And the rush of stampeded camels made a fearful din,
While the Arabs they did yell, and fiendishly did grin.

Then the gallant Marines formed the east side of the square,
While clouds of dust and smoke did darken the air,
And on the west side the Berkshire were engaged in the fight,
Firing steadily and coolly with all their might.

Still camp followers were carried along by the huge animal mass,
And along the face of the zereba 'twas difficult to pass,
Because the mass of brutes swept on in wild dismay,
Which caused the troops to be thrown into disorderly array.

Then Indians and Bluejackets were all mixed together back to back,
And for half-an-hour the fire and din didn't slack;
And none but steady troops could have stood that fearful shock,
Because against overwhelming numbers they stood as firm as a rock.

The Arabs crept among the legs of the animals without any dread,
But by the British bullets many were killed dead,
And left dead on the field and weltering in their gore,
Whilst the dying moans of the camels made a hideous roar.

Then General M'Neill to his men did say,
Forward! my lads, and keep them at bay!
Come, make ready, my men, and stand to your arms,
And don't be afraid of war's alarms!

So forward! and charge them in front and rear,
And remember you are fighting for your Queen and country dear,
Therefore, charge them with your bayonets, left and right,
And we'll soon put this rebel horde to flight.

Then forward at the bayonet-charge they did rush,
And the rebel horde they soon did crush;
And by the charge of the bayonet they kept them at bay,
And in confusion and terror they all fled away.

The Marines held their own while engaged hand-to-hand,
And the courage they displayed was really very grand;
But it would be unfair to praise one corps more than another,
Because each man fought as if he'd been avenging the death of a brother.

The Berkshire men and the Naval Brigade fought with might and main,
And, thank God! the British have defeated the Arabs once again,
And have added fresh laurels to their name,
Which will be enrolled in the book of fame.

'Tis lamentable to think of the horrors of war,
That men must leave their homes and go abroad afar,
To fight for their Queen and country in a foreign land,
Beneath the whirlwind's drifting scorching sand.

But whatsoever God wills must come to pass,
The fall of a sparrow, or a tiny blade of grass;
Also, man must fall at home by His command,
Just equally the same as in a foreign land.

BURNING OF THE EXETER THEATRE.

'TWAS in the year of 1887, which many people will long remember,
The burning of the Theatre at Exeter on the 5th of September,
Alas! that ever-to-be-remembered and unlucky night,
When one hundred and fifty lost their lives, a most agonizing sight.

The play on this night was called "Romany Rye,"
And at act four, scene third, Fire! Fire! was the cry;
And all in a moment flames were seen issuing from the stage,
Then the women screamed frantically, like wild beasts in a cage.

Then a panic ensued, and each one felt dismayed,
And from the burning building a rush was made;
And soon the theatre was filled with a blinding smoke,
So that the people their way out had to grope.

The shrieks of those trying to escape were fearful to hear,
Especially the cries of those who had lost their friends most dear;
Oh, the scene was most painful in the London Inn Square,
To see them ringing their hands and tearing their hair!

And as the flames spread, great havoc they did make,
And the poor souls fought heroically in trying to make their escape;
Oh, it was horrible to see men and women trying to reach the door!
But in many cases death claimed the victory, and their struggles were o'er.

Alas! 'twas pitiful the shrieks of the audience to hear,
Especially as the flames to them drew near;
Because on every face were depicted despair and woe,
And many of them jumped from the windows into the street below.

The crushed and charred bodies were carried into London Hotel yard,
And to alleviate their sufferings the doctors tried hard;
But, alas! their attendance on many was thrown away,
But those that survived were conveyed to Exeter Hospital without delay.

And all those that had their wounds dressed proceeded home,
Accompanied by their friends, and making a loud moan;
While the faces and necks of others were sickening to behold,
Enough to chill one's blood, and make the heart turn cold

Alas! words fail to describe the desolation,
And in many homes it will cause great lamentation;
Because human remains are beyond all identification,
Which will cause the relatives of the sufferers to be in great tribulation.

Oh, Heaven! it must have been an awful sight,
To see the poor souls struggling hard with all their might,
Fighting hard their lives to save,
While many in the smoke and burning flame did madly rave!

It was the most sickening sight that ever anybody saw,
Human remains, beyond recognition, covered with a heap of straw;
And here and there a body might be seen, and a maimed hand,
Oh, such a sight, that the most hard-hearted person could hardly withstand!

The number of the people in the theatre was between seven and eight thousand,
But, alas! one hundred and fifty by the fire have been found dead;
And the most lives were lost on the stairs leading from the gallery,
And these were roasted to death, which was sickening to see.

The funerals were conducted at the expense of the local authority,
And two hours and more elapsed at the mournful ceremony;
And at one grave there were two thousand people, a very great crowd,
And most of the men were bareheaded and weeping aloud.

Alas! many poor children have been bereft of their fathers and mothers,
Who will be sorely missed by little sisters and brothers;
But, alas! unto them they can ne'er return again,
Therefore the poor little innocents must weep for them in vain.

I hope all kind Christian souls will help the friends of the dead,
Especially those that have lost the winners of their bread;
And if they do, God surely will them bless,
Because pure Christianity is to help the widows and orphans in distress.

I am very glad to see Henry Irving has sent a hundred pound,
And I hope his brother actors will subscribe their mite all round;
And if they do it will add honour to their name,
Because whatever is given towards a good cause they will it regain.

JOHN ROUAT THE FISHERMAN.

MARGARET SIMPSON was the daughter of humble parents in the county of Ayr,
With a comely figure, and face of beauty rare,
And just in the full bloom of her womanhood
Was united to John Rouat, a fisherman good.

John's fortune consisted of his coble, three oars, and his fishing-gear,
Besides his two stout boys, John and James, he loved most dear.
And no matter how the wind might blow, or the rain pelt,
Or scarcity of fish, John little sorrow felt.

While sitting by the clear blazing hearth of his home,
With beaming faces around it, all his own.
But John, the oldest son, refused his father obedience,
Which John Rouat considered a most grievous offence.

So his father tried to check him, but all wouldn't do,
And John joined a revenue cutter as one of its crew;
And when his father heard it he bitterly did moan,
And angrily forbade him never to return home.

Then shortly after James ran away to sea without his parents' leave,
So John Rouat became morose, and sadly did grieve.
But one day he received a letter, stating his son John was dead,
And when he read the sad news all comfort from him fled.

Then shortly after that his son James was shot,
For allowing a deserter to escape, such was his lot;
And through the death of his two sons he felt dejected,
And the condolence of kind neighbours by him was rejected.

'Twas near the close of autumn, when one day the sky became o'ercast,
And John Rouat, contrary to his wife's will, went to sea at last,
When suddenly the sea began to roar, and angry billows swept along,
And, alas! the stormy tempest for John Rouat proved too strong.

But still he clutched the oars, thinking to keep his coble afloat,
When one 'whelming billow struck heavily against the boat,
And man and boat were engulfed in the briny wave,
While the Storm Fiend did roar and madly did rave.

When Margaret Rouat heard of her husband's loss, her sorrow was very great,
And the villagers of Bute were moved with pity for her sad fate,
And for many days and nights she wandered among the hills,
Lamenting the loss of her husband and other ills.

Until worn out by fatigue, towards a ruinous hut she did creep,
And there she lay down on the earthen floor, and fell asleep,
And as a herd boy by chance was passing by,
He looked into the hut and the body of Margaret he did espy.

Then the herd boy fled to communicate his fears,
And the hut was soon filled with villagers, and some shed tears.
When they discovered in the unhappy being they had found
Margaret Rouat, their old neighbour, then their sorrow was profound.

Then the men from the village of Bute willingly lent their aid,
To patch up the miserable hut, and great attention to her was paid.
And Margaret Rouat lived there in solitude for many years,
Although at times the simple creature shed many tears.

Margaret was always willing to work for her bread,
Sometimes she herded cows without any dread,
Besides sometimes she was allowed to ring the parish bell,
And for doing so she was always paid right well.

In an old box she kept her money hid away,
But being at the kirk one beautiful Sabbath day,
When to her utter dismay when she returned home,
She found the bottom forced from the box, and the money gone.

Then she wept like a child, in a hysteric fit,
Regarding the loss of her money, and didn't very long survive it.
And as she was wont to descend to the village twice a week,
The villagers missed her, and resolved they would for her seek.

Then two men from the village, on the next day
Sauntered up to her dwelling, and to their dismay,
They found the door half open, and one stale crust of bread,
And on a rude pallet lay poor Margaret Rouat cold and dead.

THE SORROWS OF THE BLIND.

Pity the sorrows of the poor blind,
For they can but little comfort find;
As they walk along the street,
They know not where to put their feet.
They are deprived of that earthly joy
Of seeing either man, woman, or boy;
Sad and lonely through the world they go,
Not knowing a friend from a foe:
Nor the difference betwixt day and night,
For the want of their eyesight;
The blind mother cannot see her darling boy,
That was once her soul's joy.
By day and night,
Since she lost her precious sight;
To her the world seems dark and drear,
And she can find no comfort here.
She once found pleasure in reading books,
But now pale and careworn are her looks.
Since she has lost her eyesight,
Everything seems wrong and nothing right.

The face of nature, with all its beauties and livery green
Appears to the blind just like a dream.
All things beautiful have vanished from their sight,
Which were once their heart's delight.
The blind father cannot see his beautiful child, nor wife,
That was once the joy of his life;
That he was wont to see at morn and night,
When he had his eyesight.
All comfort has vanished from him now,
And a dejected look hangs on his brow.
Kind Christians all, both great and small,
Pity the sorrows of the blind,
They can but little comfort find;
Therefore we ought to be content with our lot,
And for the eyesight we have got,
And pray to God both day and night
To preserve our eyesight;
And be always willing to help the blind in their distress,
And the Lord will surely bless
And guard us by night and day,
And remember us at the judgment day.

GENERAL GORDON,
THE HERO OF KHARTOUM.

ALAS! now o'er the civilised world there hangs a gloom
For brave General Gordon, that was killed in Khartoum;
He was a Christian hero, and a soldier of the Cross,
And to England his death will be a very great loss.

He was very cool in temper, generous and brave,
The friend of the poor, the sick, and the slave;
And many a poor boy he did educate,
And laboured hard to do so both early and late.

He was a man that did not care for worldly gear,
Because the living and true God he did fear;
And the hearts of the poor he liked to cheer,
And by his companions in arms he was loved most dear.

He always took the Bible for his guide,
And he liked little boys to walk by his side;
He preferred their company more so than men,
Because he knew there was less guile in them.

And in his conversation he was modest and plain,
Denouncing all pleasures he considered sinful and vain,
And in battle he carried no weapon but a small cane,
Whilst the bullets fell around him like a shower of rain.

He burnt the debtors' books that were imprisoned in Khartoum,
And freed them from a dismal prison gloom,
Those that were imprisoned for debt they couldn't pay,
And sent them rejoicing on their way.

While engaged in the Russian war, in the midst of the fight,
He stood upon a rising ground and viewed them left and right,
But for their shot and shell he didn't care a jot,
While the officers cried, Gordon, come down, or else you'll be shot.

His cane was christened by the soldiers Gordon's wand of victory,
And when he waved it the soldiers' hearts were filled with glee,
While with voice and gesture he encouraged them in the strife,
And he himself appeared to possess a charmed life.

Once when leading a storming party the soldiers drew back,
But he quickly observed that courage they did lack,
Then he calmly lighted a cigar, and turned cheerfully round,
And the soldiers rushed boldly on with a bound.

And they carried the position without delay,
And the Chinese rebels soon gave way,
Because God was with him during the day,
And with those that trust Him | of ever and aye.

He was always willing to conduct meetings for the poor,
Also meat and clothing for them he tried to procure,
And he always had little humorous speeches at command,
And to hear him deliver them it must have been grand.

In military life his equal couldn't be found,
No! if you were to search the wide world around,
And 'tis pitiful to think he has met with such a doom
By a base *traitor knave* while in Khartoum.

Yes, the black-hearted traitor opened the gates of Khartoum,
And through that the Christian hero has met his doom,
For when the gates were opened the Arabs rushed madly in,
And foully murdered him while they laughingly did grin.

But he defended himself nobly with axe and sword in hand,
But, alas! he was soon overpowered by that savage band,
And his body received a hundred spear wounds and more,
While his murderers exultingly did loudly shriek and roar.

But heaven's will, 'tis said, must be done,
And according to his own opinion his time was come;
But I hope he is now in heaven reaping his reward.
Although his fate on earth was really very hard.

I hope the people will his memory revere,
And take an example from him, and worship God in fear,
And never be too fond of worldly gear,
And walk in General Gordon's footsteps while they are here

THE BATTLE OF CRESSY.

'TWAS on the 26th of August, the sun was burning hot,
In the year of 1346, which will never be forgot,
Because the famous field of Cressy was slippery and gory,
By the loss of innocent blood which I'll relate in story.

To the field of Cressy boldly King Philip did advance,
Aided by the Bohemian Army and chosen men of France,
And treble the strength of the English Army that day,
But the lance thrusts of the English soon made them give way.

The English Army was under the command of the Prince of Wales,
And with ringing cheers the soldiers his presence gladly hails,
As King Edward spoke to the Prince, his son, and said,
My son put thou thy trust in God and be not afraid,
And he will protect thee in the midst of the fight,
And remember God always defends the right.

Then the Prince knelt on one knee before the King,
Whilst the soldiers gathered round them in a ring;
Then the King commanded that the Prince should be carefully guarded,
And if they were victorious each man would be rewarded.

These arrangements being made, the Prince rode away,
And as he rode past the ranks, his spirits felt gay;
Then he ordered the men to refresh themselves without delay,
And prepare to meet the enemy in the coming deadly fray.

Then contentedly the men seated themselves upon the grass,
And ate and drank to their hearts content, until an hour did pass;
Meanwhile the French troops did advance in disorganized masses,
But as soon as the English saw them they threw aside their glasses.

And they rose and stood in the ranks as solid as the rock,
All ready and eager to receive the enemy's shock;
And as the morning was advancing a little beyond noon,
They all felt anxious for the fight, likewise to know their doom.

Then the French considered they were unable to begin the attack,
And seemed rather inclined for to draw back;
But Count D'Alencon ordered them on to the attack,
Then the rain poured down in torrents and the thunder did crack.

Then forward marched the French with mock shrill cries,
But the English their cries most bravely defies;
And as the sun shone out in all its brilliant array,
The English let fly their arrows at them without the least dismay.

And each man fought hard with sword and lance pell mell,
And the ranks were instantly filled up as soon as a man fell;
And the Count D'Alencon, boldly charged the Black Prince,
And he cried, yield you, Sir Knight, or I'll make you wince.

Ha, by St. George! thou knowest not what thou sayest,
Therefore yield thyself, Sir Frenchman, for like an ass thou brayest;
Then planting his lance he ran at the Count without fear,
And the Count fell beneath the Black Prince's spear.
And the Black Prince and his men fought right manfully,
By this time against some forty thousand of the enemy,
Until the Prince recognised the banner of Bohemia floating in the air;
Then he cried that banner shall be mine, by St. George I do swear.

On! on! for old England, he cried, on! gentlemen on!
And spur your chargers quickly, and after them begone;
Then the foremost, a slight youth, to the Prince did reply,
My Prince, I'll capture that banner for you else I will die.
Ha! cried the Prince, is it thou my gallant Jack of Kent,
Now charge with me my brave lad for thou has been sent
By God, to aid me in the midst of the fight,
So forward, and wield your cudgel with all your might.

Then right into the midst of the Bohemian Knights they fought their way,
Brave Jack o' the Cudgel and the Prince without dismay;
And Jack rushed at the Standard Bearer without any dread,
And struck him a blow with his cudgel which killed him dead.

Then Jack bore off the Standard, to the Prince's delight,
Then the French and the Bohemians instantly took to flight;
And as the last rays of the sun had faded in the west,
The wounded and dying on both sides longed for rest.

And Philip, King of France, was wounded twice in the fray,
And was forced to fly from the field in great dismay;
And John of Hainault cried, come sire, come away,
I hope you will live to win some other day.

Then King Edward and his army, and the Prince his son,
Knelt down and thanked God for the victory won;
And the King's heart was filled with great delight,
And he thanked Jack for capturing the Bohemian Standard during the fight.

THE WRECK OF THE BARQUE "WM. PATERSON," OF LIVERPOOL.

YE landsmen all attend my verse, and I'll tell to ye a tale
Concerning the barque "Wm. Paterson "that was lost in a tempestuous gale;
She was on a voyage from Bangkok to the Clyde with a cargo of Teak wood,
And the crew numbered fifteen in all of seamen firm and good.

'Twas on the 8th of March, when a violent gale from the southward broke out,
And for nine days during tempestuous weather their ship was tossed about
By the angry sea, and the barque she sprang a leak,
Still the crew wrought at the pumps till their hearts were like to break.

And the pumps were kept constantly going for fourteen long hours,
And the poor men were drenched to the skin with sea spray showers;
Still they wrought at the pumps till they became rather clogged
Until at last the barque became thoroughly water-logged.

Oh! hard was the fate of these brave men,
While the water did rush in from stern to stem,
Poor souls 'twas enough to have driven them frantic,
To be drifting about water-logged in the Atlantic.

At last she became unmanageable and her masts had to be cut away,
Which the brave crew performed quickly without delay;
Still gales of more or less violence prevailed every day,
Whilst the big waves kept dashing o'er them, likewise the spray.

And with the fearful hurricane the deckhouse and galley were carried away,
Yet the thought of a speedy deliverance kept up their courage day by day,
And the captain prepared for the breaking up of the ship without dismay,
And to save his rations he reduced each man to two biscuits a day.

The brave heroes managed to save a pinnace about fifteen feet long,
And into it thirteen of the crew quickly and cautiously did throng,
With two bags of biscuits and a cask of water out of the tank,
And for these precious mercies, God they did thank;

Who is the giver of all good things,
And to those that put their trust in him often succour brings,
And such has been the case with these brave men at sea,
That sent Captain M'Mullan to save them and bring them to Dundee.

When once into the pinnace they improvised a sail into a tent,
Which to the crew some little shelter lent;
Still every day they were drifting towards the coast of Greenland,
Yet they hoped in God that speedy deliverance might be near at hand.

And as every day passed by they felt woe begone,
Because no sail could they see on the horizon;
And they constructed a sea anchor to keep the boat's head to sea,
And notwithstanding their hardships they stood out bravely

And on the 19th of March a ship hove in sight,
Which proved to be the "Slieve Roe" to their delight;
Then they hoisted a signal of distress when they espied the "Slieve Roe,"
But it was not seen on account of the wreck being in the water so low.

But as soon as Captain M'Mullan knew it was a signal of distress,
Then heroically and quickly his men he did address,
He cried! come my men keep the ship close to the wind,
And let's try if we can these unfortunate souls find.

And as the "Slieve Roe" to them drew near,
Poor souls they gave a hearty cheer;
Then they were immediately taken on board,
And they thanked Captain M'Mullan for saving them, likewise the Lord.

Then a crew from the "Slieve Roe" were sent away,
For the two remaining members of the crew without delay;
The Captain and a Sailor, together with a cat and a pet dog,
Which had been the companions of the sailors, and seemed as frisky as a frog.

And when they had all got safe on board,
With one accord they thanked the Lord;
And Captain M'Mullan kindly did them treat,
By giving them dry clothing and plenty of meat.

And for his kind treatment unto them he deserves great praise,
For his many manly and kindly ways,
By saving so many lives during the time he has been at sea,
And in particular for fetching the crew of the "Wm. Paterson" safe to Dundee.

HANCHEN, THE MAID OF THE MILL.

NEAR the village of Udorf, on the banks of the Rhine,
There lived a miller and his family, once on a time;
And there yet stands the mill in a state of decay,
And concerning the miller and his family, attend to my lay

The miller and his family went to Church one Sunday morn,
Leaving behind their darling child, the youngest born,
In charge of brave Hanchen, the servant maid,
A kind-hearted girl and not the least afraid.

As Hanchen was engaged preparing dinner for the family
She chanced to turn round, and there she did see
Heinrich Bottler, her lover, and she sincerely loved him,
Then she instantly got him something to eat and bade him begin.

And in the midst of her business she sat down beside him,
While he did justice to the meat and thought it no sin,
But while he was eating he let fall his knife,
Then he commanded Hanchen to pick it up or else he'd take her life.

Then as she stooped down to pick up the knife,
The villain caught her by the throat, and swore he'd take her life,
Then he drew a dagger from under his coat,
Crying tell me where your master's money is, or I'll cut your throat.

And still he threatened to kill her with the dagger in his hand,
If the poor girl didn't comply with his demand,
While in his choking grasp her breath was fleeting faster and faster,
Therefore she had no other choice but to die or betray her master.

Then she cried, mercy, for Heaven's sake let go thy hold,
And I'll tell thee where my master keeps his gold;
Then he let go his hold without delay,
And she unto him thus boldly did say.

Here, take this axe and use it, while I run upstairs,
To gather all my money, besides all my wares,
Because I'm resolved to fly along with you,
When you've robbed my master of his gold and bid France adieu.

Then deceived by her plan he allowed her to leave the room,
Telling her to make haste and come back very soon,
Then to her master's bedroom she led the way,
And showed him the coffer where her master's money lay.

Then Heinrich with the axe broke the coffer very soon,
While Hanchen instead of going upstairs to her room,
Bolted all the doors upon him without dismay,
While Heinrich was busy preparing to carry her master's money away.

Then she rushed to the mill to give the alarm,
Resolved to protect her master's money, while she could wield an arm;
And the only being in sight, was her master's boy of five years old,
Then she cried, run! run! and tell father there's a robber taking his gold.

Then the boy did as she bid him without any doubt,
And set off, running on the road she pointed out;
But at this moment, a shrill whistle made her stand aghast,
When she heard Heinrich, crying, catch that child that's running so fast.

But still the boy ran on with might and main,
Until a ruffian sprang up from the bed of a natural drain;
And snatching the boy in his arms, and hastening towards the mill,
While brave Hanchen was afraid the boy he would kill.

Then the villain came rushing with the boy towards the mill,
Crying, open the door, or the child I'll kill;
But she cried, never will I open the door to thee,
No! I will put my trust in God, and He'll save the child and me.

Then the ruffian set down the child, for a moment to look about,
Crying, open the door, or I'll fire the mill without doubt;
And while searching for combustibles, he discovered an inlet to the mill,
Saying, my pretty maid, once I get in, it's you I will kill.

Then he tied the hands and feet of the poor child,
Which caused it to scream with fear, very wild;
Then he stole back to the aperture to effect an entrance,
And when Hanchen saw him, she said now is my chance.

So the ruffian got safely in the great drum wheel,
Then Hanchen set on the engine, which made the ruffian reel;
And as he was whirled about, he screamed aloud,
And when Hanchen saw him like a rat in a trap, she felt very proud.

At length the master arrived and his family,
And when she heard his kindly voice her heart was full of glee,
Then she opened the mill door and let him in,
While her eyes with tears of joy were full to the brim.

Then the master set off the engine without delay,
And the ruffian was dragged forth while he shook with dismay,
And Heinrich and he were bound together under a strong escort,
And conveyed to Bonn Prison where villains resort.

So thus ends the story of Hanchen, a heroine brave,
That tried hard her master's gold to save,
And for her bravery she got married to the miller's eldest son,
And Hanchen on her marriage night cried Heaven's will be done.

WRECK OF THE SCHOONER "SAMUEL CRAWFORD."

'TWAS in the year of 1886, and on the 29th of November,
Which the surviving crew of the "Samuel Crawford" will long remember,
She was bound to Baltimore with a cargo of pine lumber;
But, alas! the crew suffered greatly from cold and hunger.

'Twas on December 3rd when about ten miles south-west
Of Currituck light, and scudding at her best;
That a heavy gale struck her a merciless blow,
Which filled the hearts of the crew with fear and woe.

Then the merciless snow came down, hiding everything from view,
And as the night closed in the wind tempestuous blew;
Still the brave crew reefed the spanker and all the sails,
While not one amongst them with fear bewails.

Still the gallant little schooner ploughed on the seas,
Through the blinding snow and the stormy breeze;
Until it increased to a fearful hurricane,
Yet the crew wrought manfully and didn't complain.

But during the night the wind it harder blew,
And the brave little schooner was hove to;
And on the morning of December the 4th the wind died out,
But it rent the schooner from stem to stern without any doubt.

And the seas were running mountains high,
While the poor sailors, no doubt, heaved many a sigh;
Because they must have felt cold, and the schooner sprung a leak,
Still they wrought while their hearts were like to break.

Then the wind it sprang up in terrific fury again,
But the crew baled out the water with might and main;
But still the water fast on them did gain,
Yet the brave heroes disdained to complain.

On the morning of December the 4th she was scudding before a hurricane,
And the crew were exhausted, but managed the poop to gain;
And the vessel was tossed like a cork on the wave,
While the brave crew expected to meet with a watery grave.

And huge beams and pine planks were washed overboard,
While Captain Tilton looked on and said never a word;
And the crew likewise felt quite content,
Until the fore-and-aft rigging overboard went.

Then loudly for help to God they did cry,
And to their earnest prayer He did draw nigh;
And saved them from a watery grave,
When help from Him they did crave.

Poor souls they expected to be engulfed every hour,
And to appease their hunger they made dough with salt water and flour;
And made a sort of hard cake placed over a griddle hole,
To satisfy their hunger, which, alas! is hard to thole.

And two of these cakes each man got per day,
Which the poor creatures devoured in a ravenous way;
Along with a little fresh water to wash it down,
Which they most thankfully praised God for and didn't frown.

And on the 10th of December when they had burned their last light,
The ship "Orinoco" bound for New York hove in sight;
And they were rescued safely and taken on board,
And they thanked the Captain, and likewise the Lord.

Then the Captain of the "Orinoco" ordered her to be set on fire,
Which was quickly done as he did desire;
Which caused the rescued crew to stare in amaze,
And to take the last look of their schooner in a blaze.

THE FIRST GRENADIER OF FRANCE.

'TWAS in a certain regiment of French Grenadiers,
A touching and beautiful custom was observed many years;
Which was meant to commemorate the heroism of a departed comrade,
And when the companies assembled for parade,
There was one name at roll call to which no answer was made.

It was that of the noble La Tour d'Auvergne,
The first Grenadier of France, heroic and stern;
And always at roll call the oldest sergeant stepped forward a pace,
And loudly cried, "died on the field of battle," then fell back into his place.

He always refused offers of high promotion,
Because to be promoted from the ranks he had no notion;
But at last he was in command of eight thousand men,
Hence he was called the first Grenadier of France, La Tour d'Auvergne.

When forty years of age he went on a visit to a friend,
Never thinking he would have a French garrison to defend
And while there he made himself acquainted with the country,
But the war had shifted to that quarter unfortunately.
But although the war was there he felt undaunted,
Because to fight on behalf of France was all he wanted;
And the thought thereof did his mind harass,
When he knew a regiment of Austrians was pushing on to occupy a narrow pass.

They were pushing on in hot haste and no delaying,
And only two hours distant from where the Grenadier was staying,
But when he knew he set off at once for the pass,
Determined if 'twere possible the enemy to harass.

He knew that the pass was defended by a stout tower,
And to destroy the garrison the enemy would exert all their power;
But he hoped to be able to warn the French of their danger,
But to the thirty men garrisoned there he was quite a stranger.

Still the brave hero hastened on, and when he came there,
He found the thirty men had fled in wild despair;
Leaving their thirty muskets behind,
But to defend the garrison to the last he made up his mind.

And in searching he found several boxes of ammunition not destroyed,
And for a moment he felt a little annoyed;
Then he fastened the main door, with the articles he did find,
And when he had done so he felt satisfied in mind.

Then he ate heartily of the provisions he had brought,
And waited patiently for the enemy, absorbed in thought;
And formed the heroic resolution to defend the tower,
Alone, against the enemy, while he had the power.

There the brave hero sat alone quite content,
Resolved to hold the garrison, or die in the attempt;
And about midnight his practised ear caught the tramp of feet,
But he had everything ready for the attack and complete.

There he sat and his mind absorbed in deep distress,
But he discharged a couple of muskets into the darkness;
To warn the enemy that he knew they were there,
Then he heard the Austrian officers telling their men to beware.

So until morning he was left unmolested,
And quietly till daylight the brave Grenadier rested;
But at sunrise the Austrian commander called on the garrison to surrender,
But the Grenadier replied, "never, I am its sole defender."

Then a piece of artillery was brought to bear upon the tower,
But the Grenadier from his big gun rapid fire on it did shower;
He kept up a rapid fire, and most accurate,
And when the Austrian commander noticed it he felt irate.

And at sunset the last assault was made,
Still the noble Grenadier felt not the least afraid;
But the Austrian commander sent a second summons of surrender,
Hoping that the garrison would his injunctions remember.

Then the next day at sunrise the tower door was opened wide,
And a bronzed and scarred Grenadier forth did glide;
Literally laden with muskets, and passed along the line of troops,
While in utter astonishment the Austrian Colonel upon him looks.

Behold! Colonel, I am the garrison, said the soldier proudly,
What! exclaimed the Colonel, do you mean to tell me—
That you alone have held that tower against so many men,
Yes! Colonel, I have indeed, replied La Tour d'Auvergne.

Then the Colonel raised his cap and said, you are the bravest of the brave,
Grenadier, I salute you, and I hope you will find an honourable grave;
And you're at liberty to carry the muskets along with you,
So my brave Grenadier I must bid thee adieu.

At last in action the brave solider fell in June 1800,
And the Emperor Napoleon felt sorry when he heard he was dead;
And he commanded his regiment to remember one thing above all,
To cry out always the brave Grenadier's name at the roll call.

THE TRAGIC DEATH OF THE REV. A.H. MACKONOCHIE.

FRIENDS of humanity, of high and low degree,
I pray ye all come listen to me;
And truly I will relate to ye,
The tragic fate of the Rev. Alexander Heriot Mackonochie.

Who was on a visit to the Bishop of Argyle
For the good of his health, for a short while;
Because for the last three years his memory had been affected,
Which prevented him from getting his thoughts collected.

'Twas on Thursday, the 15th of December, in the year of 1887,
He left the Bishop's house to go and see Loch Leven;
And he was accompanied by a little skye terrier and a deerhound,
Besides the Bishop's two dogs, that knew well the ground.

And as he had taken the same walk the day before,
The Bishop's mind was undisturbed and easy on that score;
Besides the Bishop had been told by some men,
That they saw him making his way up a glen.

From which a river flows down with a mighty roar,
From the great mountains of the Mamore;
And this route led him towards trackless wastes eastward,
And no doubt to save his life he had struggled very hard.

And as Mr Mackonochie had not returned at dinner time,
The Bishop ordered two men to search for him, which they didn't decline;
Then they searched for him along the road he should have returned,
But when they found him not, they sadly mourned.

And when the Bishop heard it, he procured a carriage and pair,
While his heart was full of woe, and in a state of despair;
He organised three search parties without delay,
And headed one of the parties in person without dismay.

And each party searched in a different way,
But to their regret at the end of the day;
Most unfortunately no discovery had been made,
Then they lost hope of finding him, and began to be afraid.

And as a last hope, two night searches were planned,
And each party with well lighted lamps in hand
Started on their perilous mission, Mr Mackonochie to try and find,
In the midst of driving hail, and the howling wind.

One party searched a distant sporting lodge with right good will,
Besides through brier, and bush, and snow, on the hill;
And the Bishop's party explored the Devil's Staircase with hearts full of woe,
A steep pass between the Kinloch hills, and the hills of Glencoe.

Oh! it was a pitch dark and tempestuous night,
And the searchers would have lost their way without lamp light;
But the brave searchers stumbled along for hours, but slow,
Over rocks, and ice, and sometimes through deep snow.

And as the Bishop's party were searching they met a third
    party from Glencoe side,
Who had searched bracken and burn, and the country wide;
And sorrow was depicted in each one's face,
Because of the Rev. Mr Mackonochie they could get no trace

But on Saturday morning the Bishop set off again,
Hoping that the last search wouldn't prove in vain;
Accompanied with a crowd of men and dogs,
All resolved to search the forest and the bogs.

And the party searched with might and main,
Until they began to think their search would prove in vain;
When the Bishop's faithful dogs raised a pitiful cry,
Which was heard by the searchers near by.

Then the party pressed on right manfully,
And sure enough there were the dogs guarding the body of Mackonochie;
And the corpse was cold and stiff, having been long dead,
Alas! almost frozen, and a wreath of snow around the head.

And as the searchers gathered round the body in pity they did stare,
Because his right foot was stained with blood, and bare;
But when the Bishop o'er the corpse had offered up a prayer,
He ordered his party to carry the corpse to his house on a bier.

So a bier of sticks was most willingly and quickly made,
Then the body was most tenderly upon it laid;
And they bore the corpse and laid inside the Bishop's private chapel,
Then the party took one sorrowful look, and bade the corpse farewell.

THE BURNING OF THE STEAMER "CITY OF MONTREAL."

A SAD tale of the sea I will relate, which will your hearts appal,
Concerning the burning of the steamship "City of Montreal,"
Which had on board two hundred and forty-nine souls in all,
But, alas! a fearful catastrophe did them befall.

The steamer left New York on the 6th August with a general cargo,
Bound for Queenstown and Liverpool also;
And all went well until Wednesday evening the 10th,
When in an instant an alarming fire was discovered at length.

And most of the passengers had gone to their berths for the night,
But when the big bell rang out, oh! what a pitiful sight;
To see mothers and their children crying, was most heartrending to behold,
As the blinding smoke began to ascend from the main hold.

And the smoke before long drifted down below,
Which almost choked the passengers, and filled their hearts with woe;
Then fathers and mothers rushed madly upon the deck,
While the crew were struggling manfully the fire to check.

Oh, it was a soul-harrowing and horrible sight,
To see the brave sailors trying hard with all their might;
Battling furiously with the merciless flames—
With a dozen of hose, but still the fire on them gains.

At length it became apparent the steamer couldn't be saved,
And the passengers were huddled together, and some of them madly raved;
And the family groups were most touching to see,
Especially husbands and wives embracing each other tenderly.

The mothers drew their little ones close to them,
Just like little lambs huddled together in a pen;
While the white foaming billows was towering mountains high,
And one and all on God for protection did cry.

And when the Captain saw the steamer he couldn't save,
He cried, come men, prepare the boats to be launched on the briny wave;
Be quick, and obey my orders, let each one bear a hand—
And steer the vessel direct for Newfoundland.

Then the men made ready the boats, which were eight on board,
Hurriedly and fearlessly with one accord;
And by eight o'clock on Thursday morning, everything was ready
For the passengers to leave the burning steamer that was rolling unsteady.

Then Captain Land on his officers loudly did call,
And the cheery manliness of him inspired confidence in all;
Then he ordered the men to lower the boats without delay,
So the boats were launched on the stormy sea without dismay.

Then women and children were first put into them,
Also a quantity of provisions, then followed the men;
And as soon as the boats were loaded they left the steamer's side,
To be tossed to and fro on the ocean wide.

And just as they left the burning ship, a barque hove in sight,
Which filled the poor creatures hearts with delight;
And the barque was called the "Trebant," of Germany,
So they were all rescued and conveyed to their homes in safety.

But before they left the barque, they thanked God that did them save
From a cold and merciless watery grave;
Also the Captain received their thanks o'er and o'er,
Whilst the big waves around the barque did sullenly roar.

So good people I warn ye all to be advised by me,
To remember and be prepared to meet God where'er ye may be;
For death claims his victims, both on sea and shore,
Therefore be prepared for that happy land where all troubles are o'er.

THE WRECK OF THE WHALER "OSCAR."

'TWAS on the 1st of April, and in the year of Eighteen thirteen,
That the whaler "Oscar" was wrecked not far from Aberdeen;
'Twas all on a sudden the wind arose, and a terrific blast it blew,
And the "Oscar" was lost, and forty-two of a gallant crew.

The storm burst forth with great violence, but of short duration,
And spread o'er a wide district, and filled the people's hearts with consternation,
And its effects were such that the people will long mind,
Because at Peterhead the roof was torn off a church by the heavy wind.

The "Oscar" joined other four ships that were lying in Aberdeen Bay,
All ready to start for Greenland without delay,
While the hearts of each ship's crew felt light and gay,
But, when the storm burst upon them, it filled their hearts with dismay.

The wind had been blowing westerly during the night,
But suddenly it shifted to the North-east, and blew with all its might,
And thick and fast fell the blinding snow,
Which filled the poor sailors' hearts with woe.

And the "Oscar" was exposed to the full force of the gale,
But the crew resolved to do their best, allowing they should fail,
So they weighed anchor, and stood boldly out for sea,
While the great crowds that had gathered cheered them encouragingly.

The ill-fated "Oscar," however, sent a boat ashore
For some of her crew that were absent, while the angry sea did roar,
And 'twas with great difficulty the men got aboard,
And to make the ship alright they wrought with one accord.

Then suddenly the wind shifted, and a treacherous calm ensued,
And the vessel's deck with snow was thickly strewed;
And a heavy sea was running with a strong flood tide,
And it soon became apparent the men wouldn't be able the ship to guide.

And as the "Oscar" drifted further and further to leeward,
The brave crew tried hard her backward drifting to retard,
But all their efforts proved in vain, for the storm broke out anew,
While the drifting snow hid her from the spectators' view.

And the position of the "Oscar" was critical in the extreme,
And as the spray washed o'er the vessel, O what a soul-harrowing scene!
And notwithstanding the fury of the gale and the blinding snow,
Great crowds watched the "Oscar" as she was tossed to and fro.

O heaven! it was a most heart-rending sight
To see the crew struggling against wind and blinding snow with all their might,
While the mighty waves lashed her sides and angry did roar,
Which to their relatives were painful to see that were standing on shore,

All eagerly watching her attempt to ride out the storm,
Especially their friends and relatives, who seemed very forlorn.
Because the scene was awe-inspiring and made them stand aghast,
For every moment seemed to be the "Oscar's" last.

Oh! it was horrible to see the good ship in distress,
Battling hard against wind and tide to clear the Girdleness.
A conspicuous promontory on the south side of Aberdeen Bay,
Where many a stout ship and crew have gone down passing that way.

At last the vessel was driven ashore in the bay of Greyhope,
And the "Oscar" with the elements no longer could cope.
While the big waves lashed her furiously, and she received fearful shocks,
Until a mighty wave hurled her among large boulders of rocks.

And when the vessel struck, the crew stood aghast,
But they resolved to hew down the mainmast,
Which the spectators watched with eager interest,
And to make it fall on the rocks the brave sailors tried their best.

But, instead of falling on the rocks, it dropped into the angry tide,
Then a groan arose from those that were standing on the shore side;
And the mainmast in its fall brought down the foremast,
Then all hope of saving the crew seemed gone at last.

And a number of the crew were thrown into the boiling surge below,
While loud and angry the stormy wind did blow,
And the good ship was dashed to pieces from stern to stem,
Within a yard or two of their friends, who were powerless to save them.

Oh! it was an appalling sight to see the "Oscar" in distress,
While to the forecastle was seen clinging brave Captain Innes
And five of a crew, crying for help, which none could afford,
Alas! poor fellows, crying aloud to God with one accord!

But their cry to God for help proved all in vain,
For the ship and men sank beneath the briny main,
And out of a crew of forty-four men, only two were saved,
But, landsmen, think how manfully that unfortunate crew behaved.

And also think of the mariners while you lie down to sleep,
And pray to God to protect them while on the briny deep,
For their hardships are many, and hard to endure,
There's only a plank between them and a watery grave, which
    makes their lives unsure.

JENNY CARRISTER,
THE HEROINE OF LUCKNOW-MINE.

A HEROIC story I will unfold,
Concerning Jenny Carrister, a heroine bold,
Who lived in Australia, at a gold mine called Lucknow,
And Jenny was beloved by all the miners, somehow.

Jenny was the only daughter of the old lady who owned the mine—
And Jenny would come of an evening, like a gleam of sunshine,
And by the presence of her bright face and cheery voice,
She made the hearts of the unlucky diggers rejoice.

There was no pride about her, and day after day,
She walked with her young brother, who was always gay,
A beautiful boy he was, about thirteen years old,
And Jenny and her brother by the miners were greatly extolled.

Old Mrs Carrister was every inch a lady in her way,
Because she never pressed any of the miners that weren't able to pay
For the liberty of working the gold-field,
Which was thirty pounds per week for whatever it might yield.

It was in the early part of the year 1871,
That Jack Allingford, a miner, hit on a plan,
That in the mine, with powder, he'd loosen the granite-bound face,
So he selected, as he thought, a most suitable place.

And when all his arrangements had been made,
He was lowered down by a miner that felt a little afraid,
But most fortunately Jenny Carrister came up at the time,
Just as Jack Allingford was lowered into the mine.

Then she asked the man at the windlass if he'd had any luck,
But he picked up a piece of candle and then a match he struck;
Then Jenny asked the miner, What is that for?
And he replied to blast the mine, which I fear and abhor.

Then with a piece of rope he lowered the candle and matches into the mine,
While brave Jenny watched the action all the time;
And as the man continued to turn round the windlass handle,
Jenny asked him, Isn't it dangerous to lower the matches and candle?

Then the man replied, I hope there's no danger, Jenny my lass,
But whatsoever God has ordained will come to pass;
And just as he said so the windlass handle swung round,
And struck him on the forehead, and he fell to the ground.

And when Jenny saw the blood streaming from the fallen man's head,
She rushed to the mouth of the shaft without any dread,
And Jenny called loudly, but received no reply,
So to her brother standing near by she heaved a deep sigh.

Telling him to run for assistance, while she swung herself on to the hand-rope,
Resolved to save Jack Allingford's life as she earnestly did hope;
And as she proceeded down the shaft at a quick pace,
The brave heroine knew that death was staring her in the face

And the rope was burning her hands as she descended,
But she thought if she saved Jack her task would be ended;
And when she reached the bottom of the mine she did not hesitate,
But bounded towards Jack Allingford, who was lying seemingly inanimate.

And as she approached his body the hissing fuse burst upon her ears,
But still the noble girl no danger fears;
While the hissing of the fuse was like an engine grinding upon her brain,
Still she resolved to save Jack while life in her body did remain.

She noticed a small jet of smoke issuing from a hole near his head,
And if he'd lain a few seconds longer there he'd been killed dead,
But God had sent an angel to his rescue,
For seizing him by the arms his body to the air shaft she drew.

It was a supernatural effort, but she succeeded at last,
And Jenny thanked God when the danger was past,
But at the same instant the silence was broke
By a loud explosion, which soon filled the mine with smoke.

But, oh, God be thanked! the greatest danger was past,
But when Jenny saw Jack Allingford, she stood aghast,
Because the blood was issuing from his nose and ears,
And as Jenny viewed his wounds she shed many tears.

But heroic Jenny was not one of the fainting sort,
For immediately to the mouth of the mine she did resort,
And she called loudly for help, the noble lass,
And her cry was answered by voices above at the windlass.

So there were plenty to volunteer their services below,
And the rope was attached to the windlass, and down they did go,
And Jack Allingford and Jenny were raised to the top,
While Jenny, noble soul, with exhaustion was like to drop.

And when the miners saw her safe above there was a burst of applause,
Because she had rescued Jack Allingford from death's jaws;
So all ye that read or hear this story, I have but to say,
That Jenny Carrister was the noblest heroine I've ever heard of in my day.

THE HORRORS OF MAJUBA.

'TWAS after the great Majuba fight:
And the next morning, at daylight,
Captain Macbean's men were ordered to headquarters camp,
So immediately Captain Macbean and his men set out on tramp.

And there they were joined by the Blue Jackets and 58th men,
Who, for unflinching courage, no man can them condemn;
And that brave little band was commissioned to bury their dead,
And the little band numbered in all about one hundred.

And they were supplied with a white flag, fit emblem of death,
Then they started off to O'Neill's farm, with bated breath,
Where their comrades had been left the previous night,
And were lying weltering in their gore, oh! what a horrible sight.

And when they arrived at the foot of Majuba Hill,
They were stopped by a Boer party, but they meant no ill,
Who asked them what they wanted without dismay,
And when they said, their dead, there was no further delay.

Then the brave heroes marched on, without any dread,
To the Hill of Majuba to collect and bury their dead;
And to see them climbing Majuba it was a fearful sight,
And much more so on a dark pitch night.

And on Majuba there was a row of dead men,
Numbering about forty or fifty of them;
There were also numbers of wounded men lying on the ground,
And when Captain Macbean's party gazed on them their sorrow was profound.

Oh, heaven! what a sight of blood and brains!
While the grass was red all o'er with blood-stains;
Especially at the edge of the Hill, where the 92nd men were killed,
'Twas there that the eyes of Macbean's party with tears filled,

When they saw their dead and dying comrades in arms,
Who were always foremost in the fight during war's alarms;
But who were now lying dead on Majuba Hill,
And, alas! beyond the aid of all human skill.

They then went about two hundred yards down the Hill,
And collected fourteen more bodies, which made their blood run chill;
And, into one grave, seventy-five bodies they buried there,
All mostly 92nd men, who, I hope, are free from all care.

Oh! think of that little gallant British band,
Who, at Majuba, made such a heroic stand,
And, take them altogether, they behaved like brave men,
But, alas! they were slaughtered like sheep in a pen.

Poor fellows! there were few of them left to retire,
Because undauntedly they faced that murderous fire,
That the mighty host poured in upon them, left and right,
From their numerous rifles, day and night.

The conduct of the 92nd was most brave throughout,
Which has always been the case, without any doubt;
At least, it has been the case in general with the Highland Brigade,
Because in the field they are the foremost, and seldom afraid.

And to do the British justice at Majuba they behaved right, well,
But by overwhelming numbers the most of them fell,
Which I'm very sorry to relate,
That such a brave little band met with such a fate.

The commanders and officers deserve great praise,
Because they told their men to hold Majuba for three days;
And so they did, until the most of them fell,
Fighting nobly for their Queen and country they loved right well.

But who's to blame for their fate I'm at a loss to know,
But I think 'twas by fighting too numerous a foe;
But there's one thing I know, and, in conclusion, will say,
That their fame will be handed down to posterity for many a day!

THE MIRACULOUS ESCAPE OF ROBERT ALLAN, THE FIREMAN.

'TWAS in the year of 1888, and on October the fourteenth day,
That a fire broke out in a warehouse, and for hours blazed away;
And the warehouse, now destroyed, was occupied by the Messrs
    R. Wylie, Hill & Co.,
Situated in Buchanan Street, in the City of Glasgow.

The flames burst forth about three o'clock in the afternoon,
And intimation of the outbreak spread very soon;
And in the spectators' faces were depicted fear and consternation;
While the news flew like lightning to the Fire Brigade Station.

And when the Brigade reached the scene of the fire,
The merciless flames were ascending higher and higher,
Raging furiously in all the floors above the street,
And within twenty minutes the structure was destroyed by the burning heat.

Then the roof fell in, pushing out the front wall,
And the loud crash thereof frightened the spectators one and all,
Because it shook the neighbouring buildings to their foundation,
And caused throughout the City a great sensation.

And several men were injured by the falling of the wall,
And as the bystanders gazed thereon, it did their hearts appal;
But the poor fellows bore up bravely, without uttering a moan,
And with all possible speed they were conveyed home.

The firemen tried to play upon the building where the fire originated,
But, alas! their efforts were unfortunately frustrated,
Because they were working the hose pipes in a building occupied by
    Messrs Smith & Brown,
But the roof was fired, and amongst them it came crashing down.

And miraculously they escaped except one fireman,
The hero of the fire, named Robert Allan,
Who was carried with the debris down to the street floor,
And what he suffered must have been hard to endure.

He travelled to the fire in Buchanan Street
On the first machine that was ordered, very fleet,
Along with Charles Smith and Dan. Ritchie,
And proceeded to Brown & Smith's buildings that were burning furiously.

And in the third floor of the building he took his stand
Most manfully, without fear, with the hose in his hand,
And played on the fire through a window in the gable
With all his might, the hero, as long as he was able.

And he remained there for about a quarter of an hour,
While from his hose upon the building the water did pour,
When, without the least warning, the floor gave way,
And down he went with it: oh, horror! and dismay!

And with the debris and flooring he got jammed,
But Charlie Smith and Dan. Ritchie quickly planned
To lower down a rope to him, without any doubt,
So, with a long pull and a strong pull, he was dragged out.

He thought he was jammed in for a very long time,
For, instead of being only two hours jammed, he thought 'twas months nine,
But the brave hero kept up his spirits without any dread,
Then he was taken home in a cab, and put in bed.

Oh, kind Christians! think of Robert Allan, the heroic man,
For he certainly is a hero, deny it who can?
Because, although he was jammed, and in the midst of the flame,
He tells the world fearlessly he felt no pain.

The reason why, good people, he felt no pain
Is because he put his trust in God, to me it seems plain.
And in conclusion, I most earnestly pray,
That we will all put our trust in God, night and day.

And I hope that Robert Allan will do the same,
Because He saved him from being burnt while in the flame;
And all those that trust in God will do well,
And be sure to escape the pains of hell.

THE BATTLE OF SHINA, IN AFRICA, FOUGHT IN 1800.

KING SHUAC, the Giant of Mizra, war did declare
Against Ulva, King of Shina, telling him to prepare
And be ready for to meet him in the fight,
Which would commence the next morning before daylight.

When King Ulva heard the news, he told his warriors to prepare,
Then suddenly the clatter of arms sounded in the night air;
And the pale beams of the moon shone on coats of mail,
But not one bosom beneath them with fear did quail.

And bugles rang out their hoarse call,
And armed men gathered quickly, not in dread of their downfall;
For King Ulva resolved to go and meet Shuac,
So, by doing so, King Ulva's men courage didn't lack.

Therefore, the temple was lighted up anew,
And filled with armed warriors, bold and true;
And the King stood clad in his armour, and full of pride,
As he gazed upon his warriors, close by his side.

And he bowed himself to the ground,
While there was a deep silence around;
And he swore, by his false god of the all-seeing eye,
That he would meet Shuac, King of Mizra, and make him fly.

And I swear that in Shina peace shall remain,
And whatever thou desireth, supreme one, will not be in vain;
For thou shalt get what thou considereth to be most fit,
Though it be of my own flesh and blood, I swear it.

Then, when all was in readiness, they marched before the dawn,
Sixty thousand in number, and each a picked man;
And they marched on silently to take Shuac's army by surprise,
And attack him, if possible, before sunrise.

King Shuac's army were about one hundred thousand strong,
And, when King Ulva heard so, he cried, We'll conquer them ere long,
Therefore, march on, brave men, we'll meet them before daybreak,
So, be resolute and conquer, and fight for Shina's sake.

Within a mile of the enemy's camp they lay all night,
Scarcely taking well-earned repose, they were so eager for the fight;
And when the morning broke clear and cloudless, with a burning sun,
Each warrior was wishing that the fight was begun.

And as the armies neared one another, across the fertile land,
It was a most imposing sight, and truly grand,
To see the warriors clad in armour bright,
Especially the form of Shuac, in the midst of the fight.

The royal guard, forming the vanguard, made the first attack,
Under the command of King Ulva, who courage didn't lack;
And cries of "King Ulva!" and "King Shuac!" rent the air,
While Shuac cried, I'll burn Shina to the ground, I now do swear!

King Shuac was mounted on a powerful steed,
Which pressed its way through the ranks with lightning speed;
And with its hoofs the earth it uptears,
Until, with a bound, it dashes through the ranks of opposing spears.

Then the two Kings met each other at last,
And fire flashed from their weapons, and blows fell fast;
But Shuac was the strongest of the two,
But King Ulva was his match with the club, Ulva knew.

Then, with his club, he gave Shuac a blow, which wounded him deep,
Crying out, Shuac, thy blood is deserting thee! thou art a sheep!
Cried Ulva, dealing him another fearful blow,
Then Shuac raised his club and rushed on his foe.

Then his blow fell, and knocked Ulva's club from his hand,
While both armies in amazement stand
To watch the hand-to-hand fight,
While Shuac's warriors felt great delight.

But there chanced to be a Scotchman in Ulva's army
That had a loaded pistol, and he fired it immediately,
And shot King Shuac through the head,
And he toppled over to the ground killed stone dead!

Then the men of Mizra laid down their arms and fled
When they saw that their King was killed dead;
Then King Ulva said to the Scotchman, I am thy servant for ever,
For to thee I owe my life, and nought but death will us sever.

THE COLLISION IN THE ENGLISH CHANNEL.

'TWAS on a Sunday morning, and in the year of 1888,
The steamer "Saxmundham," laden with coal and coke for freight,
Was run into amidships by the Norwegian barque "Nor,"
And sunk in the English Channel, while the storm fiend did roar.

She left Newcastle on Friday, in November, about two o'clock,
And proceeded well on her way until she received a shock;
And the effects of the collision were so serious within,
That, within twenty minutes afterwards, with water she was full to the brim.

The effects of the collision were so serious the water couldn't be staunched,
So immediately the "Saxmundham's" jolly-boat was launched;
While the brave crew were busy, and loudly did clatter,
Because, at this time, the stem of the steamer was under water.

Then the bold crew launched the lifeboat, without dismay,
While their hearts did throb, but not a word did they say;
Then they tried to launch the port lifeboat, but in that they failed,
Owing to the heavy sea, so their sad fate they bewailed.

Then into the jolly-boat and lifeboat jumped fifteen men in all,
And immediately the steamer foundered, which did their hearts appal,
As the good ship sank beneath the briny wave,
But they thanked God fervently that did them save.

Oh! it was a miracle how any of them were saved,
But it was by the aid of God, and how the crew behaved;
Because God helps those that help themselves,
And those that don't try to do so are silly elves.

So the two boats cruised about for some time,
Before it was decided to pull for St. Catherine;
And while cruising about they must have been ill,
But they succeeded in picking up an engineer and fireman, also Captain Milne.

And at daybreak on Sunday morning the men in the lifeboat
Were picked up by the schooner "Waterbird" as towards her they did float,
And landed at Weymouth, and made all right
By the authorities, who felt for them in their sad plight.

But regarding the barque "Nor," to her I must return,
And, no doubt, for the drowned men, many will mourn;
Because the crew's sufferings must have been great,
Which, certainly, is soul-harrowing to relate.

The ill-fated barque was abandoned in a sinking state,
But all her crew were saved, which I'm happy to relate;
They were rescued by the steamer "Hagbrook" in the afternoon,
When after taking to their boats, and brought to Portland very soon.

The barque "Nor" was bound from New York to Stettin,
And when she struck the "Saxmundham," oh! what a terrible din!
Because the merciless water did rush in,
Then the ship carpenters to patch the breach did begin.

But, alas! all their efforts proved in vain,
For still the water did on them gain;
Still they resolved to save her whatever did betide,
But, alas! the ill-fated "Nor" sank beneath the tide.

But thanks be to God, the major part of the men have been saved,
And all honour to both crews that so manfully behaved;
And may God protect the mariner by night and by day
When on the briny deep, far, far away!

THE WRECK OF THE STEAMER "STORM QUEEN."

YE landsmen, all pray list to me,
While I relate a terrible tale of the sea,
Concerning the screw-steamer "Storm Queen,"
Which was wrecked, alas! a most heart-rending scene.

From Sebastopol, with a cargo of grain, she was on her way,
And soon after entering the Bay of Biscay,
On the 21st of December, they experienced a fearful storm,
Such as they never experienced since they were born.

The merciless sea was running mountains high,
And to save themselves from a watery grave manfully they did try;
But the vessel became unmanageable, but still they worked away,
And managed to launch two small boats without dismay.

They wrought most manfully and behaved very well,
But a big wave smashed a small boat before they left the vessel;
Still the Captain Mr Jaques and five of the crew
Clung to the "Storm Queen" until she sank beneath the waters blue.

While the sea lashed itself into white foam and loudly did roar,
And with a gurgling sound the big waves covered the vessel o'er,
So perished Captain Jaques and five of the crew,
Who stuck to the vessel, as brave sailors would do.

But before the vessel sank, a raft was made
And a few men got on it, who were not afraid;
And, oh! it was enough to make one's blood to freeze
To see them jumping off the steamer into the yawning seas!

So they were tossed about on the big billows the whole night,
And beneath the big waves they were engulfed before daylight;
But twenty-two that reached the boats were saved in all
By the aid of God, on whom they did call.

And on the next morning before daylight
The Norwegian barque "Guluare" hove in sight;
Then they shouted, and pulled towards her with all their might,
While the seas were running high, oh! what a fearful sight!

The poor souls were prevented from getting alongside
Of the barque "Guluare," by the heavy seas and tide;
And as the boats drew near the barque the storm increases,
Until the boats struck against her and were dashed to pieces.

It was almost beyond human efforts with the storm to cope,
But most fortunately they were hauled on board by a rope,
While the big waves did lash the barque all over;
But by a merciful providence they were landed safely at Dover.

The survivors when rescued were in a destitute state,
But nevertheless they seemed resigned to their fate;
And they thanked God that did them save
Most timely from a cold and watery grave.

And during their stay in Dover they received kind treatment,
For which the poor creatures felt very content;
And when they had recovered from their ills they met at sea,
The authorities sent them home to their own country.

But as for Captain Jaques, few men like him have been,
Because he couldn't be persuaded to desert the "Storm Queen,"
As he declared he wouldn't leave her whatever did betide,
So the brave hero sank with her beneath the waters wide.

THE PENNSYLVANIA DISASTER.

'TWAS in the year of 1889, and in the month of June,
Ten thousand people met with a fearful doom,
By the bursting of a dam in Pennsylvania State,
And were burned, and drowned by the flood—oh! pity their fate!

The embankment of the dam was considered rather weak,
And by the swelled body of water the embankment did break,
And burst o'er the valley like a leaping river,
Which caused the spectators with fear to shiver.

And on rushed the mighty flood, like a roaring big wave,
Whilst the drowning people tried hard their lives to save;
But eight thousand were drowned, and their houses swept away,
While the spectators looked on, stricken with dismay.

And when the torrent dashed against the houses they instantly toppled o'er,
Then many of the houses caught fire, which made a terrific roar;
And two thousand people, by the fire, lost their lives,
Consisting of darling girls and boys, also men and their wives.

And when the merciless flood reached Johnstown it was fifty feet high,
While, in pitiful accents, the drowning people for help did cry;
But hundreds of corpses, by the flood, were swept away,
And Johnstown was blotted out like a child's toy house of clay.

Alas! there were many pitiful scenes enacted,
And many parents, for the loss of their children, have gone distracted,
Especially those that were burned in the merciless flame,
Their dear little ones they will never see again.

And among the sad scenes to be witnessed there,
Was a man and his wife in great despair,
Who had drawn from the burning mass a cradle of their child,
But, oh, heaven! their little one was gone, which almost drove them wild.

Oh, heaven! it was a pitiful and a most agonising sight,
To see parents struggling hard with all their might,
To save their little ones from being drowned,
But 'twas vain, the mighty flood engulfed them, with a roaring sound.

There was also a beautiful girl, the belle of Johnstown,
Standing in bare feet, on the river bank, sad and forlorn,
And clad in a loose petticoat, with a shawl over her head,
Which Was all that was left her, because her parents were dead.

Her parents were drowned, and their property swept away with the flood,
And she was watching for them on the bank where she stood,
To see if they would rise to the surface of the water again,
But the dear girl's watching was all in vain.

And as for Conemaugh river, there's nothing could it surpass,
It Was dammed up by a wall of corpses in a confused mass;
And the charred bodies could be seen dotting the burning debris,
While the flames and sparks ascended with a terrific hiss.

The pillaging of the houses in Johnstown is fearful to describe,
By the Hungarians and ghouls, and woe betide
Any person or party that interfered with them,
Because they were mad with drink, and yelling like tigers in a den.

And many were to be seen engaged in a hand-to-hand fight,
And drinking whisky, and singing wild songs, oh! what a shameful sight!
But a number of the thieves were lynched and shot
For robbing the dead of their valuables, which will not be forgot.

Mrs Ogle, like a heroine, in the telegraph office stood at her post,
And wired words of warning, else more lives would have been lost;
Besides she was warned to flee, but from her work she wouldn't stir,
Until at last the merciless flood engulfed her.

And as for the robbery and outrage at the hands of the ghouls,
I must mention Clara Barton and her band of merciful souls,
Who made their way fearlessly to the Wounded in every street,
And the wounded and half-crazed survivors they kindly did treat.

Oh, heaven! it was a horrible sight, which will not be forgot,
So many people drowned and burned—oh! hard has been their lot!
But heaven's will must be done, I'll venture to say,
And accidents will happen until doomsday!

THE SPRIG OF MOSS.

There lived in Munich a poor, weakly youth,
But for the exact date, I cannot vouch for the truth,
And of seven of a family he was the elder,
Who was named, by his parents, Alois Senefelder.

But, poor fellow, at home his father was lying dead,
And his little brothers and sisters were depending upon him for bread,
And one evening he was dismissed from his employment,
Which put an end to all his peace and enjoyment.

The poor lad was almost mad, and the next day
His parent's remains to the cemetery were taken away;
And when his father was buried, distracted like he grew,
And he strolled through the streets crying, What shall I do!

And all night he wandered on sad and alone,
Until he began to think of returning home,
But, to his surprise, on raising his head to look around,
He was in a part of the country which to him was unknown ground.

And when night came on the poor lad stood aghast,
For all was hushed save the murmuring of a river which flowed past;
And the loneliness around seemed to fill his heart with awe,
And, with fatigue, he sat down on the first stone he saw.

And there resting his elbows and head on his knees,
He sat gazing at the running water, which did him please;
And by the light of the stars which shone on the water blue,
He cried, I will drown myself, and bid this harsh world adieu.

Besides, I'm good for nothing, to himself he said,
And will only become a burden to my mother, I'm afraid;
And there, at the bottom of that water, said he
From all my misfortunes death will set me free.

But, happily for Alois, more pious thoughts rushed into his mind,
And courage enough to drown himself he couldn't find,
So he resolved to go home again whatever did betide,
And he asked forgiveness of his Creator by the river side.

And as he knelt, a few incoherent words escaped him,
And the thought of drowning himself he considered a great sin,
And the more he thought of it, he felt his flesh creep,
But in a few minutes he fell fast asleep.

And he slept soundly, for the stillness wasn't broke,
And the day was beginning to dawn before he awoke;
Then suddenly he started up as if in a fright,
And he saw very near him a little stone smooth and white,

Upon which was traced the delicate design of a Sprig of Moss,
But to understand such a design he was at a loss,
Then he recollected the Sprig of Moss lying on the stone,
And with his tears he'd moistened it, but it was gone.

But its imprint was delicately imprinted on the stone;
Then, taking the stone under his arm, he resolved to go home,
Saying, God has reserved me for some other thing,

And with joy he couldn't tell how he began to sing.
And on drawing near the city he met his little brother,
Who told him his uncle had visited his mother,
And on beholding their misery had left them money to buy food,
Then Alois cried, Thank God, the news is good!

Then 'twas on the first day after Alois came home,
He began the printing of the Sprig of Moss on the stone;
And by taking the impressions of watch-cases he discovered, one day,
What is now called the art of Lithography.

So Alois plodded on making known his great discovery,
Until he obtained the notice of the Royal Academy,
Besides, he obtained a gold Medal, and what was more dear to his heart,
He lived to see the wide extension of his art.

And when life's prospects may at times appear dreary to ye,
Remember Alois Senefelder, the discoverer of Lithography,
How God saved him from drowning himself in adversity,
And I hope ye all will learn what the Sprig of Moss teaches ye.

And God that made a way through the Red Sea,
If ye only put your trust in Him, He will protect ye,
And light up your path, and strew it with flowers,
And be your only Comforter in all your lonely hours.

Echo Library
www.echo-library.com

Echo Library uses advanced digital print-on-demand technology to build and preserve an exciting world class collection of rare and out-of-print books, making them readily available for everyone to enjoy.

Situated just yards from Teddington Lock on the River Thames, Echo Library was founded in 2005 by Tom Cherrington, a specialist dealer in rare and antiquarian books with a passion for literature.

Please visit our website for a complete catalogue of our books, which includes foreign language titles.

The Right to Read

Echo Library actively supports the Royal National Institute of the Blind's Right to Read initiative by publishing a comprehensive range of large print and clear print titles.

Large Print titles are in 16 point Tiresias font as recommended by the RNIB.

Clear Print titles are in 13 point Tiresias font and designed for those who find standard print difficult to read.

Customer Service

If there is a serious error in the text or layout please send details to feedback@echo-library.com and we will supply a corrected copy. If there is a printing fault or the book is damaged please refer to your supplier.

Lightning Source UK Ltd.
Milton Keynes UK
UKOW04f0224021117
312028UK00001B/103/P